Reflections

by Jim Branch

Introduction

When writing a book, I am told, it is wise to have your audience firmly in your mind—to clearly see and know the target at which you are aiming... Oops.

That is definitely not the case with this book. I just started reading the gospel of Mark with some friends and began to write. I began to write my thoughts, and my reflections, and the movement of the Spirit within me as I both read and prayed. This book is simply a result of that process. It is a record of how God was speaking to me through his word at that particular time; which is one of the most beautiful aspects of God's Word—it is alive. It is always speaking, always guiding, always molding.

So who is this book for? This book is for anyone and everyone. It is for anyone and everyone who longs for a deep and intimate relationship with Jesus. It is for anyone and everyone who desires to spend daily time with the God who made them uniquely and loves them deeply. It is for anyone and everyone who wants to hear a word from the God who desperately wants to speak a word to His beloved children. So whether you have been following Jesus for three days or for three decades, it is my hope that this book is for you. I pray that it offers you a fruitful space to listen to the voice of the Spirit through the Word of God. And I pray that, as we journey together, you will come face-to-face with God in a way that will grow your faith in Him and deepen your affection for Him.

A Few Suggestions

This book moves to a very definite rhythm—one that has existed for centuries. The rhythm involves four particular movements: *reading, reflecting, responding,* and *resting.* You will find these movements to be very similar to that of a dance; back and forth, to and fro, in and out—following the Spirit as he leads. It is a dance that is intended not to restrict, but to offer a structure that might actually allow you to hear God's voice a little more clearly. My hope is that it will put you in tune with God in such a way that it allows you to move to the rhythm of His Spirit as he leads you in a dance of life and joy and peace. And that through dancing in this way with your God, your daily time with him, as well as your very life, will be completely transformed.

So begin your time each day, therefore, by *reading* the Scripture for that day. As you read, do so slowly, with an attentiveness to what the words are saying; or rather what the Spirit of God is saying to you through the words. It might actually be helpful to read the passage several times; or maybe to read it out loud. And always remember, what you are reading is the *living and active* Word of God (Heb. 4:12) and He has something specific that He wants to say to you.

Next, spend some time *reflecting* on what you have read. As you reflect, pay careful attention to certain words or images that might capture you or stand out for some reason. As you are drawn to something specific within the text, begin to ask God what it is about that particular word or image that he wants you to see. If what you are reading is a gospel encounter, you might want to imagine yourself being one of the characters in the scene. What would you be thinking? What would you be feeling? What are your joys? What are your fears? What are your deepest longings? What do you need most from Jesus? Consider how that particular character is like you or what God might be saying to you through the encounter. Again, read the verses several times and allow the words to both work on you and move in you. In the words of writer Macrina Wiederkehr, "wear them like a robe."

After you have spent some time in reflection, turn your attention to any *response* that seems to be welling up within you. This response can take many forms. For example, you might want to respond by recording your thoughts, prayers, and feelings in a journal each day. This is a great way to monitor or track the movement of God in your life and heart. You may want to write a poem, or a prayer, or a story. Or you may want to draw a picture that symbolizes something that God is saying to you or doing in you. There are also exercises and questions along the way that should help in this process. Use them only as they are helpful. If the Spirit is leading you some other direction, by all means follow Him.

Finally, *rest*. That's right; simply rest in God's presence. Just be with Him. Sit with Him. Savor and enjoy Him, the same way you would enjoy loved ones around a table, totally contented, after a fabulous meal. And hopefully as we journey together, your soul will be both formed and transformed into the very image of Jesus.

Blessings,

JB

One

Read:
The beginning of the gospel about Jesus Christ, The Son of God. (Mark 1:1)

Reflect:
The beginning. What a great place to start. Beginnings are wonderful things. They are so full of possibility, and expectation, and hope. A beginning is a blank page just waiting to be filled. A beginning is that point in time where everything is fresh and new. A beginning is that place where everything is filled with a sense of adventure and anticipation.

Every good story has a beginning. Your story had one; as did mine. And as we *begin* this journey together over these next days and weeks, Mark welcomes us by inviting us to join in a beginning—the beginning of the story of Jesus, the Son of God. Jesus, the visible expression of the invisible God (Colossians 1:15). Jesus, the One that reflects God's own glory and represents God's being exactly (Hebrews 1:3 NLT). Jesus, the Word of God that became flesh and made his dwelling among us (John 1:14). Jesus, the Alpha and Omega, the Beginning and the End (Revelation 21:6).

In Jesus, Paul tells us, God gives us a full and complete expression of himself (Colossians 2:9 JBP). The God who made all things becomes one of us; to show us his incredible love, to show us the depths of his heart, to show us what he is really like. It is simply unbelievable! It is truly Good News (*gospel*).

Reflect on the word *beginning.*
What is significant to you about it?
Think about the beginnings in your life.
What was unique about them? What were they like?
How have they shaped and formed you?
In what ways are you at a beginning right now?
How do you feel about that?
When did your story with Jesus begin? How?
Where do you need a new beginning?

Respond:
Talk with God about your beginnings. Ask him to move and to act in them. Thank God for the beginning of your story with him and for the people he used to draw your heart to himself.

Rest:
Just be with God for a few minutes in silence.

Two

Read:

> *It is written in Isaiah the Prophet:*
> *"I will send my messenger ahead of you,*
> *who will prepare the way"*
> *a voice of one calling in the desert,*
> *'Prepare the way for the Lord,*
> *make straight paths for him.' "*

And so John came, baptizing in the desert region and preaching a baptism of repentance for the forgiveness of sins. The whole Judean countryside and all the people of Jerusalem went out to him. Confessing their sins, they were baptized by him in the Jordan River. John wore clothing made of camel's hair, with a leather belt around his waist, and he ate locusts and wild honey. And this was his message: "After me will come one more powerful than I, the thongs of whose sandals I am not worthy to stoop down and untie. I baptize you with water, but he will baptize you with the Holy Spirit." (Mark 1:2-8)

Reflect:
Dear John,
　　Thank you for preparing the way
　　　　rather than trying to be the way.
　　Thank you for stepping aside
　　　　rather than stepping in front of.
　　Thank you for pointing to Jesus
　　　　rather than pointing to yourself.
　　Thank you for letting go
　　　　rather that holding on.
　　Thank you for decreasing
　　　　rather than increasing.
　　I pray that God would give me both the courage and the willingness to follow your example—both in my life and in my ministry.

A couple of questions for reflection:
Who pointed you to Jesus? How?
Who are you currently pointing to Him?
What does John teach you about relationship with God? What does he teach you about ministry?

Respond:
Write your own letter to John the Baptist telling him what his life and his example have told you about your own.

Rest:
Just be with God for a few minutes in silence.

Three

Read:
At that time Jesus came from Nazareth in Galilee and was baptized by John in the Jordan. As Jesus was coming up out of the water, he saw heaven being torn open and the Spirit descending on him like a dove. And a voice came from heaven: "You are my Son, whom I love; with you I am well pleased."

At once the Spirit sent him out into the desert, and he was in the desert forty days, being tempted by Satan. He was with the wild animals, and the angels attended him. (Mark 1:9-13)

Reflect:
Beloved—it is truly one of the most important words in all of the spiritual life. So important, in fact, that it is the word God chooses to give to Jesus as he steps out of anonymity and into the wilderness. It is a word of affection, a word of identity, a word of intimacy, and a word of hope. It is a word that offers an anchor to the heart and soul. It is also a word that will sustain Jesus, not only through his forty days of trials and temptations in the wilderness, but ultimately all the way to the cross.

Beloved—it is also the word God gives to each of us as we journey through this life; this life where we are often tempted to believe that we have no value or worth. If there was ever one word that, if we truly believed it, would change everything about us, this is it. If somehow we could possibly believe that we are completely and totally loved and accepted by the God who created us—apart from performance or appearance—we would be truly free. If somehow we could possibly believe that God calls us His Beloved. That is our name. Jesus believed it and it made all of the difference. Could it not do the same for us?

Do you truly believe you are God's beloved?
How does this knowledge offer you freedom? Identity? Hope?

Respond:
We all tend to live out of the name that we believe to be most true about us. What name are you most tempted to believe is really true about you? Write it down. Consider the ways in which that name has affected the way you live your life—the way you interact with people.

Now write down the word Beloved. That is the name that is most true about you. That is your true identity in Christ. You are the Beloved of

God. Repeat that name in your heart over and over and let I become a part of you.

Rest:
In the stillness, simply rest in God's love for you.

Four

Read:
After John was put in prison, Jesus went into Galilee, proclaiming the good news of God. "The time has come," he said. "The kingdom of God is near. Repent and believe the good news!" (Mark 1:14-15)

Reflect:
It's time! You can almost hear the excitement, and anticipation, and hope in the very words themselves. They are words that make your heart skip a beat and make your soul stand on tip-toe. They are words that are filled with yearning—for whatever it is you have been waiting for and hoping for and longing for to finally arrive.

Have you ever found yourself waiting for it "to be time?" Maybe there's something you are waiting for right now, something that simply can't get here soon enough. Like waiting for Christmas morning to see what is in those wonderfully wrapped gifts beneath the tree.

It's time! God's people had been waiting. It had been so long—400 years—since God's people had seen his hand or heard his voice. They had waited and waited for his coming, for him to end his silence, for him to walk among his people.

It's time! There are actually two words for *time* in the Greek. One of them, *chronos,* is quantitative and thus has to do with measurable time—hours and minutes and seconds. It is the word we would use if someone were to ask us what time it was. The other word is *kairos* and is qualitative, having to do more with the fullness of time; as in whether or not something is ripe or ready. It is the word that would be used if someone were to ask if it was time for a tree to bloom, or time to pick a fruit from the vine. The second word is the one that Jesus utters in this case, as he comes on the scene in Galilee after thirty years in obscurity and near anonymity.

Jesus had finally arrived and it was not just good news, it was great news! All the waiting and longing and anticipation were finally over. The kingdom had come. The King had arrived to live among his people—to deliver them from slavery and oppression and suffering and despair and fear and sin and death. Finally, God had come. Finally, *it was time!*

Where in your life are you waiting for/longing for God to

show up?
What do the words *It's time* do in you right now? Why?

Respond:
Take some time at the end of your day today to reflect back upon it.
Prayerfully walk back through your day and be attentive to how God might
have been present in ways that you might not have noticed at the time.
Write them down and give him thanks for His presence and care.

Rest:
Just be with God and thank him for his presence and companionship in
your life.

Five

Read:
*As Jesus walked beside the Sea of Galilee, he saw Simon and his brother
Andrew casting a net into the lake, for they were fishermen. "Come, follow
me," Jesus said, "and I will make you fishers of men." At once they left
their nets and followed him. When he had gone a little farther, he saw
James son of Zebedee and his brother John in a boat, preparing their nets.
Without delay he called them, and they left their father Zebedee in the boat
with the hired men and followed him.   (Mark 1:16-20)*

Reflect:
Follow me. Words that were simple enough, but incredibly profound
and demanding at the same time. Jesus calls these men to follow
him...and they do! They up and leave their families and their jobs and their
homes, and even their very lives, to follow him. Why? What would make
them be willing to drop everything and follow him? What would make you
be willing to do that? What was it about him?

Was it something about his spirit? Something about the way he spoke
and moved and listened and cared? Or was it something about the quality
of life and love and peace that came up from deep within him? Was it
something in his eyes—the way he looked at you—that was able to see to
the very core of your being? Was it something in his voice—the way he
spoke to you—that spoke to your deepest longings and insecurities and
fears? Was it something in the way he walked—with great intention and
purposefulness in every stride—like a man on a mission? Maybe it was a
combination of them all. But whatever the reason; they followed. They left
their old lives behind and began brand new lives under his direction. No
longer were they merely trying to catch fish, now they were trying to catch
men.

What makes you willing to follow someone?
What makes you resistant?
Where do you sense a willingness to follow Jesus in
    your life right now?
Where is there resistance?

Respond:
Listen carefully to the ways and the places in your life that Jesus is calling
you to follow him. What will it mean to put yourself under his direction?
What might you have to leave behind?

Rest:
In the stillness, rest in God's direction of your life. He alone is worthy of
our trust.

Six

Read:
*They went to Capernaum, and when the Sabbath came, Jesus went into
the synagogue and began to teach. The people were amazed at his
teaching, because he taught them as one who had authority, not as the
teachers of the law. Just then a man in their synagogue who was
possessed by an evil spirit cried out, "What do you want with us, Jesus of
Nazareth? Have you come to destroy us? I know who you are--the Holy
One of God!" "Be quiet!" said Jesus sternly. "Come out of him!" The evil
spirit shook the man violently and came out of him with a shriek. The
people were all so amazed that they asked each other, "What is this? A
new teaching--and with authority! He even gives orders to evil spirits and
they obey him." News about him spread quickly over the whole region of
Galilee. (Mark 1:21-28)*

Reflect:
   Religious leaders are a dime a dozen. You see them everywhere—on
the street corner, in the pulpit, on cable TV. Just turn on the television and
you can find ten different preachers to listen to at any given moment; each
with his or her own message, his or her own style, and his or her own
agenda. All of them claiming to have a word from the Lord, but most falling
far short of their claims.
   It was no different in Jesus' day. The religious leaders were a vocal
bunch, always the experts in the ways of God. They were always creating
rule after rule that the people couldn't possibly keep—loading them down
with heavy burdens of guilt and ought and shame. *Shoulding on them*, as
one of my friends likes to call it.

Then Jesus comes on the scene, and enters the synagogue, and begins to teach. When the people hear his voice they recognize a power and an authority that they had never heard before. In fact his words brought life—i.e., changed lives—not death; something they had never seen (or heard) before. In fact, whatever it was that he had, they wanted it. None of the other religious leaders had it. He was completely different; in tone and in quality and in depth and in every other way. And the people were absolutely amazed.

Respond:
Spend some time journaling about how God has changed your life in the past year. What words has he spoken to you that have had the power and authority to transform you? To give you life, hope, and freedom?

Now consider the parts of your life where you still long for transformation. Ask God to speak a word of power and authority into those parts of your life as well. Do you believe he can? Do you believe he will? Do you really want to be changed?

Rest:
Psalm 62:11-12 tells us that God is both strong and loving. Therefore, He is worthy of our faith and trust. Rest in God's strong and loving arms.

Seven

Read:
As soon as they left the synagogue, they went with James and John to the home of Simon and Andrew. Simon's mother-in-law was in bed with a fever, and they told Jesus about her. So he went to her, took her hand and helped her up. The fever left her and she began to wait on them. (Mark 1:29-31)

Reflect:
Not only did the *words* of Jesus have the power to transform, but so did his *touch*. And wherever he went he was constantly reaching out and touching people—with a genuinely healing touch. In this instance he reaches out and touches Simon's mother-in-law. And as soon as he takes her by the hand she is healed. Did you notice that? He took her by the hand.

What a sweet and intimate picture; the God of all creation reaching out and taking one of his beloved children by the hand. It seems to shout to us all: *"I am the God who is near, not the god who is far away. I long to be near to you, and touch you, and know you deeply and intimately. I long to make you whole, for it is by my touch that you are brought to life. I care about you. I care about your life. I care about your sorrows. I love you* with an everlasting love. Let me touch every area of your life, and your heart, and your soul with my strong and tender hands. So that you may be healed, so that you may be restored to the wholeness and the beauty for which you were created. And how I long for you to put your hand in mine and live life in intimate relationship with me. Let me guide your steps; let me carry your joys and your sorrows; let me be your closest friend, your lover, your protector, your provider, your healer...and your God."

Respond:
Trace your hand on a piece of paper. At the top of the page write, "My life is in Your hands." Now, inside the hand, write down all of your concerns and worries; all of your sorrows and pains; all of your hopes and dreams--giving each one of them over to His love and care and control as you do. With each item that you write down repeat the phrase at the top of the page..."Lord Jesus, my life is in Your hands."

Rest:
Spend some time simply resting in God hands or allowing his hands to rest on you, whichever seems most appropriate at this moment.

Eight

Read:
That evening after sunset the people brought to Jesus all the sick and demon-possessed. The whole town gathered at the door, and Jesus healed many who had various diseases. He also drove out many demons, but he would not let the demons speak because they knew who he was. Very early in the morning, while it was still dark, Jesus got up, left the house and went off to a solitary place, where he prayed. Simon and his companions went to look for him, and when they found him, they exclaimed: "Everyone is looking for you!" Jesus replied, "Let us go somewhere else--to the nearby villages--so I can preach there also. That is why I have come." So he traveled throughout Galilee, preaching in their synagogues and driving out demons. (Mark 1:32-39)

Reflect:
The whole town had gathered at the doorstep—the hurting, the broken, the crippled, the possessed, the lame. And one-by-one he looked them in the eye, and reached out his hand, and spoke words of healing and of life. Each had come with a particular need and each had been met right in the midst of their pain. Each had come wounded and broken and each had left healed and whole. It must've taken all night. His disciples must've watched in wonder and amazement. He was the talk of the town.

And as they watched the last of their guests vanish into the now early morning darkness, I'll bet they were all pretty exhausted—especially Jesus. They probably planned to sleep in the next morning and then get up and walk around town to hear the stories of the incredible happenings of the night they had just witnessed.

But that wasn't Jesus' plan at all. Instead, he was up early, *while it was still dark.* He just couldn't stay away from his Father. He would rather be with his Father than do anything else—including sleep. His time with God was what gave him life, and energy, and refreshment, and peace. So while everyone else was asleep, he rose, and went off into the quiet, to be with his Father. You see it is much easier to hear God's voice in the silence than it is in the noise and the chaos.

When the disciples got up they noticed that his bed was empty. He wasn't anywhere to be found, so they went out to look for him. After all, there were places to go and things to do and people to see. They had an agenda for the day ahead. And when they finally did find him and told him about their plans, he met them with plans of his own—because Jesus had spent the early morning hours listening to God. He had received God's agenda for the day ahead; to go somewhere else—to another town—that they too might be touched by the hand of God.

Jesus gives us a great picture of what it means to order our lives around the voice and will of the Father—to be with Him, to listen to Him, and then to follow Him.

Respond:
Spend some time today just being with God—listening to Him. Listen to Him in His Word. Listen to Him in your Spirit (His Spirit that lives in you). Listen to Him in creation. And as the day unfolds, listen to Him in the interactions you have with the people in your life and world. Ask Him to set the agenda for the day ahead. What do you think He wants for you and from you this day?

Rest:
In the stillness and quiet of this moment, rest in His presence.

Nine

Read:
A man with leprosy came to him and begged him on his knees, "If you are willing, you can make me clean." Filled with compassion, Jesus reached out his hand and touched the man. "I am willing," he said. "Be clean!" Immediately the leprosy left him and he was cured. Jesus sent him away at once with a strong warning: "See that you don't tell this to anyone. But go, show yourself to the priest and offer the sacrifices that Moses

commanded for your cleansing, as a testimony to them." Instead he went out and began to talk freely, spreading the news. As a result, Jesus could no longer enter a town openly but stayed outside in lonely places. Yet the people still came to him from everywhere. (Mark 1:40-45)

Reflect:
It started out as a couple of spots on his hand, not even noticeable really. But then it began to spread. And as it did, he began to be suspicious that it was something more than just a rash. Before too long he was sure. It had to be leprosy. Now his mission was to hide it for as long as he possibly could—the law was so strict and so harsh on lepers. His life would never be the same again once they all knew. No one could see it. No one could find out. Before long everyone would know, but for now all he wanted to do was squeeze out a few more days, or weeks, of normalcy; because after that it was a life of pain and suffering, of loneliness and isolation. The disease would spread and slowly eat away at his flesh, literally making it rot and fall off the bone. There was no disease that was more brutal...or more feared.

That was months ago. And now the disease was full blown—it had attacked every part of his body. It was literally impossible to hide its ugliness. He was fighting a losing battle and he knew it. His life would never be the same again. At least that's what he thought...until he heard about Jesus. "Everything he touches," people were saying, "is transformed."

"But," he thought to himself, "Do you think he would really touch me...a leper?" And to his amazement...and his delight...the answer was a resounding "Yes!"

Respond:
Spend some time journaling about the following questions:
What parts of yourself do you try to hide from others?
What would happen if those parts were "found out?"
How do you think God feels about them?
How do you think God feels about you?
Can you possibly believe that God would be willing to
    put his clean hands on those ugly places and heal
    them?

Rest:
Place your hidden flaws and fears in the loving and transforming hands of Jesus...and rest in his love. Yes, he is willing.

Ten

Read:
A few days later, when Jesus again entered Capernaum, the people heard that he had come home. So many gathered that there was no room left, not even outside the door, and he preached the word to them. Some men came, bringing to him a paralytic, carried by four of them. Since they could not get him to Jesus because of the crowd, they made an opening in the roof above Jesus and, after digging through it, lowered the mat the paralyzed man was lying on. When Jesus saw their faith, he said to the paralytic, "Son, your sins are forgiven." Now some teachers of the law were sitting there, thinking to themselves, "Why does this fellow talk like that? He's blaspheming! Who can forgive sins but God alone?" Immediately Jesus knew in his spirit that this was what they were thinking in their hearts, and he said to them, "Why are you thinking these things? Which is easier: to say to the paralytic, 'Your sins are forgiven,' or to say, 'Get up, take your mat and walk'? But that you may know that the Son of Man has authority on earth to forgive sins..." He said to the paralytic, "I tell you, get up, take your mat and go home." He got up, took his mat and walked out in full view of them all. This amazed everyone and they praised God, saying, "We have never seen anything like this!" (Mark 2:1-12)

Reflect:
A great habit to cultivate, as we look at the Scriptures each day, is to try and put ourselves in the shoes of those inside the story: to see through their eyes, to hear through their ears, to feel with their hearts. Because by doing so, somehow the story comes to life for each of us—telling us what the words and actions of Jesus have to say specifically to us in our own story.

Having said that, read the story again, this time with the eyes of your heart, and try to imagine what it must have been like to be the paralytic. What was he feeling? What was he thinking? What were his greatest hopes and what were his deepest fears?

What did he say when his friends scooped him up and set out on their journey? What did he really think would happen? Was he discouraged when they could not get in the door, or was he somehow relieved? Was he afraid when they decided to head up to the roof, or was he excited?

And imagine what it would have been like to be in the crowd, or to be the owner of the house, or to be one of the Pharisees, or one of the disciples. Each of them has their own perspective—their own agenda, their own hopes, their own fears...and their own beliefs. And each of them has their own message for us.

At this moment, the people in the story that I'm most drawn to are the four—the carriers. What an amazing group! How deeply they must have cared for their paralyzed friend. And how hopeful they must have been to take him, despite all obstacles, to the feet of Jesus; firmly believing that if they got him there Jesus would do the rest.

We are not told how far they had come. We are not told what it might have cost them to make the journey; in terms of time and money and time away from families and loved ones—as well as time away from work. It seems that no cost was too great, and no distance was too far, and no obstacle was too big. They were a determined bunch—determined to get their friend to the feet of Jesus. And it was when Jesus saw *their* faith that he said to the man, "Get up. Pick up your mat and walk."

What about you? Who were the people that carried your mat? Who were the ones who picked you up and believed? Who were the ones that overcame all of your objections and complaints? Who were the ones that, in spite of all the obstacles and all the discouragements, placed you before the Savior?

And who might you need to be making the journey for? Who has God put in your life that desperately needs to know the great affection of their Heavenly Father? Who in your life needs the healing touch of Jesus, but can't or won't make the journey on their own?

Will you pick them up? Will you care enough to carry them to the feet of Jesus? Will you truly believe that if you get them there, he will do the rest?

Respond:
Write a letter to those who carried your mat, thanking them for their efforts and for their love. Thank them that their faith was a substantial part of your "getting up."

Now spend some time thinking about who God is calling you to carry to the feet of Jesus. Write their names down. Hold them before the Father in prayer and ask God for the strength and the courage and the faith to carry their mat, whatever that may mean.

Rest:
Spend some time in God's presence simply resting in your salvation.

Eleven

Read:
Once again Jesus went out beside the lake. A large crowd came to him, and he began to teach them. As he walked along, he saw Levi son of Alphaeus sitting at the tax collector's booth. "Follow me," Jesus told him, and Levi got up and followed him. While Jesus was having dinner at Levi's house, many tax collectors and "sinners" were eating with him and his disciples, for there were many who followed him. When the teachers of the law who were Pharisees saw him eating with the "sinners" and tax collectors, they asked his disciples: "Why does he eat with tax collectors

and 'sinners'?" On hearing this, Jesus said to them, "It is not the healthy who need a doctor, but the sick. I have not come to call the righteous, but sinners." (Mark 2:13-17)

Reflect:
I don't know about you, but I've never really cared much for people that "have it all figured out." You know, those folks that seem to be way too sure of themselves. As a matter of fact, I try to avoid those people at every opportunity. Maybe it's because I have a hard time believing that life is that tidy. My experience has been just the opposite—that life is actually pretty messy. The funny thing is that it was the "messy people" that seemed to be most drawn to Jesus; as well as the ones he seemed most drawn to. And it was the "tidy people,"—those that were the "experts" in both life and in religion—who seemed to continually have the biggest problem with him.

There's something about a God who is most drawn to the messy and broken, the hurting and unsure, that I really like. There is something about a God who would rather be at a party with the tattered than at a religious function with the "flawless" that gives a lift to my heart and soul. And there is something about a God who is continually questioning and challenging the "perfect" while pursuing and caring tenderly for the imperfect that makes me smile more than just a little. I guess it is because it gives me hope in the midst of the struggle.

How does it make you feel?

Respond:
Read the Scripture again and put yourself in the story. Where are you? Who do you most relate to? How are you like Levi and his friends? How are you like the Pharisees? What encourages or disturbs you about that? Why? What is God's response to both of these places in you?

Rest:
Invite Jesus into the house of your soul for the next few minutes. Be with him there and enjoy his company.

Twelve

Read:
Now John's disciples and the Pharisees were fasting. Some people came and asked Jesus, "How is it that John's disciples and the disciples of the Pharisees are fasting, but yours are not?" Jesus answered, "How can the guests of the bridegroom fast while he is with them? They cannot, so long as they have him with them. But the time will come when the bridegroom will be taken from them, and on that day they will fast. "No one sews a

patch of unshrunk cloth on an old garment. If he does, the new piece will pull away from the old, making the tear worse. And no one pours new wine into old wineskins. If he does, the wine will burst the skins, and both the wine and the wineskins will be ruined. No, he pours new wine into new wineskins." (Mark 2:18-22)

Reflect:
Old or *new?* If you had to choose, which one would you pick? Which one are you more drawn to? Why? What word or image does each one bring to mind? How does each make you feel?

When something is old it is broken-in, familiar, and comfortable. Conversely, it is also worn down and worn out, and in all likelihood, lifeless and dead. To borrow a worn out phrase, it is what it is. It cannot make itself new again, can't restore itself; it has no hope. It has no choice but to continue its downward spiral.

On the other hand, the new may be less comfortable, at first, and completely unfamiliar; but it is also clean and fresh and unsoiled. It has plenty of life ahead of it and is filled with potential and possibility. The new has time and room to change and grow and mature.

Jesus seemed to have a definite preference toward the new—new life, new birth, new covenant, making all things new. Could it be that he was well aware that the old stood for bondage and habit and ritual and decay? Could it be that deep in his heart he knew that we all feel so worn down and worn out? Could it be that he knew each of us, deep down inside, has a desire for a fresh start—a clean slate? Could it be that his chief desire was to do away with the old and bring about the new?

He seemed to know and understand that the old and the new could not coexist—they couldn't stand side by side. A thing cannot be new and old at the same time; it must be one or the other. A new patch will tear an old garment and new wine will burst old wineskins. We can't have them both. It is not possible to have a little bit of new while holding onto our favorite things of old.

But that is what we are constantly trying to do: trying to patch up our old, worn out ways with a small piece of new cloth. We want a little bit of the new, without having to completely let go of the old. But we must realize that just a patch will not do, we must get a whole new garment. Likewise, we can't contain the fullness and new life (wine) of the Spirit in our tired old hearts and souls—they just can't hold it. The new Spirit will burst it wide open.

Although we try and try, we simply can't have them both. We must choose one or the other—new life through Jesus or old ways without Him. Which one will it be?

Respond:
Reflect on the following questions and respond to them in your journal. What old holes are you trying to patch with a little bit of new? What new

life is growing in you that your old life simply can't contain? Where are you struggling with the old? Where are you longing for the new? Ask God to make you new.

Rest:
Spend some time resting in the fact that it is God at work in you to will and to act according to His good pleasure. It is His work and He will do it.

Thirteen

Read:
One Sabbath Jesus was going through the grainfields, and as his disciples walked along, they began to pick some heads of grain. The Pharisees said to him, "Look, why are they doing what is unlawful on the Sabbath?" He answered, "Have you never read what David did when he and his companions were hungry and in need? In the days of Abiathar the high priest, he entered the house of God and ate the consecrated bread, which is lawful only for priests to eat. And he also gave some to his companions." Then he said to them, "The Sabbath was made for man, not man for the Sabbath. So the Son of Man is Lord even of the Sabbath." (Mark 2:23-28)

Reflect:
When you hear the word *Sabbath* what thoughts and images come to your mind? Or if someone were to ask you to define the word, what would you say? Would your thoughts have more to do with what you couldn't do or with what you could do? Does the word fill you with dread or with anticipation? Do you think of it as a gift or as an obligation?

The truth is that from the very beginning the Sabbath was intended to be a gift—something that was woven into the fabric of our created being. For six days we spend ourselves in constant exhale—working, serving, doing, co-creating. And the Sabbath is our opportunity to stop and take a deep breath—to inhale.

It is an opportunity to rest from all our efforts and to renew our life and strength and energy. As a matter of fact the Hebrew word for Sabbath (*shabbat*) means to *rest* or *cease* or *end*. So, in its deepest sense, the Sabbath is an invitation: an invitation to stop, to refresh, to re-create. It is an invitation to focus on God and the intimacy of our relationship with him—to dance with Him, to play with Him, to sing to Him, to rest in Him, to be with Him. Hopefully these things are woven into the fabric of each of our days, but on the Sabbath we are given the opportunity to immerse ourselves completely in them—completely in Him! It is what we were created for.

In fact, when we choose to not observe the Sabbath it actually tears at the fabric of our created being, as well as our created rhythm and order, because we were made in such a way that our hearts and souls demand a regular period of rest and reflection; of refreshment and renewal.

So pick a day of the week and receive the gift of time and space that God has planned for you. Because, as Jesus said, "The Sabbath was made for man, not man for the Sabbath."

Respond:
Practice observing the Sabbath this week. Select a day (Sabbath is usually practiced from sundown to sundown) and plan to enter into a time of rest, reflection, and restoration in communion with God. Don't necessarily concentrate of what you will not do during the Sabbath, but on the things God might be inviting you to participate in (rest, prayer, reflection, silence, sleep, a walk, good conversation) as a part of observing the Sabbath.

After you have taken your Sabbath day, take some time and reflect of the experience. What was it like? What gave you life? What was difficult? Why?

Rest:
For the next ten minutes take a mini-Sabbath. Simply breathe, inhale, rest in silence in God's presence. Does this make you look forward to your Sabbath day or make you anxious about it?

Fourteen

Read:
Another time he went into the synagogue, and a man with a shriveled hand was there. Some of them were looking for a reason to accuse Jesus, so they watched him closely to see if he would heal him on the Sabbath. Jesus said to the man with the shriveled hand, "Stand up in front of everyone." Then Jesus asked them, "Which is lawful on the Sabbath: to do good or to do evil, to save life or to kill?" But they remained silent. He looked around at them in anger and, deeply distressed at their stubborn hearts, said to the man, "Stretch out your hand." He stretched it out, and his hand was completely restored. Then the Pharisees went out and began to plot with the Herodians how they might kill Jesus. (Mark 3:1-6)

Reflect:
We're not told his name, or his age, or anything else about him. All we're told is that he had a shriveled hand. It has to make you wonder how it got that way, or if it had been like that since he was born. One thing is for sure, when you have something that is not what it's supposed to be, you take great lengths to hide it. Maybe he was easily able to conceal it under the sleeve of his robe, or maybe he had to work a little harder—be a little

more creative. But you can be sure he didn't just let it hang out in the open for all to see.

Aren't we all like that? Don't we all have parts of ourselves that are not what they were intended to be; parts that are twisted and distorted—or shriveled? It might be something outward and noticeable, or it might be something deep inside. But whatever it is, you can bet that our deepest desire is to keep it hidden. Because it is something that causes us a great deal of shame; something that we are embarrassed about and do not want others to see or to know about. So, just like the man with the shriveled hand, we hide it.

Luckily, however, (both for us and for him) we can't hide it from Jesus. He sees right *into* us. He sees us to the very core. He sees the twistedness, and the distortedness, and the ugliness. And He knows. He knows the fear. He knows the pain. He knows the loneliness. And he cares…deeply. He longs to touch and transform; to renew and restore that which is shriveled and broken. He longs to turn it into something that is healed and whole and new.

Respond:
Write a little in your journal about the following questions:

Is there anything that you are hiding? Do you have any secrets? Are there any places within you that are shriveled or twisted? Things that are not the way they were intended to be? How does it make you feel that Jesus knows? That he cares? That he longs to restore? What would it mean for you to "stretch out your hand?"

Rest:
Place your "shriveled hand" in God's care this day. Rest in the fact that he cares—and that he longs to heal and to restore.

Fifteen

Read:
Jesus withdrew with his disciples to the lake, and a large crowd from Galilee followed. When they heard all he was doing, many people came to him from Judea, Jerusalem, Idumea, and the regions across the Jordan and around Tyre and Sidon. Because of the crowd he told his disciples to have a small boat ready for him, to keep the people from crowding him. For he had healed many, so that those with diseases were pushing forward to touch him. Whenever the evil spirits saw him, they fell down before him and cried out, "You are the Son of God." But he gave them strict orders not to tell who he was. (Mark 3:7-12)

Reflect:

Jesus and his disciples withdrew from the crowds, yet the crowds continued to come after them. They were simply relentless. What was it about him that made them come after Jesus wherever he went? Did they come after him because of what they had heard? Did they come after him because of what they had seen? Maybe it was simply because they knew in their hearts that *He* was what they desperately needed.

They needed *his* touch. They needed *his* care. They needed *his* love. They needed the hope *he* alone was able to provide. Because, in the core of their being, there was a deep longing for the health and the wholeness and the peace that only *he* could provide. It was this longing that drove them, and this longing that made them relentlessly pursue him—that made them *push forward to touch him*. Because wherever he went, he transformed everyone he touched. And ultimately this is what they were all yearning for—transformation.

What about you? What do you long for? Where are you *pushing forward to touch him*? In what part of your life (or heart) do you desperately desire healing? Wholeness? Transformation?

Respond:

Spend some time in prayer right now telling God your deepest longings and your deepest needs. Tell him where you desire his touch. Tell him where you yearn for his presence. Write these prayers in your journal.

Rest:

Take a few minutes and simply rest in his presence. Knowing that he is touching and holding your life in ways you can't even fully understand.

Sixteen

Read:

Jesus went up on a mountainside and called to him those he wanted, and they came to him. He appointed twelve—designating them apostles—that they might be with him and that he might send them out to preach and to have authority to drive out demons. These are the twelve he appointed: Simon (to whom he gave the name Peter); James son of Zebedee and his brother John (to them he gave the name Boanerges, which means Sons of Thunder); Andrew, Philip, Bartholomew, Matthew, Thomas, James son of Alphaeus, Thaddaeus, Simon the Zealot and Judas Iscariot, who betrayed him. (Mark 3:13-19)

Reflect:

If we pay careful attention to the words above, we can see two distinct movements that are vital to the spiritual life. These movements are intimately connected and, therefore, always need to be held together. They are movements that are as inseparable as breathing out and breathing in. They are the movements of being *calling toward* and being *sent out*.

Being *calling toward* is the spiritual inhale. It is the part of the spiritual life that is meant to give us life within. God calls us towards himself, to be in intimate relationship with him; to know him and to be known. It is what gives us our sense of identity and value and worth. Mark tells us that Jesus called those *he wanted …that they might be with him*. Is that not unbelievable? God wants us! And what he wants is for to *be with* him. God issues us a divine invitation to become his very own. Because what God really wants, first and foremost, is just to *be with us*! He wants our hearts, he wants our souls, and he wants our very lives. He wants our attention, and our time, and our energy. He wants our faith, and our hope, and our love. He wants every bit of us!

The second movement is being *sent out*. It is the spiritual exhale. This movement is meant to give us our sense of mission and direction and purpose. It tells us how, and to whom, we are to be given on God's behalf. It reminds us that we are not our own. Before all else, we belong to him and therefore, our lives are to be used for his purposes. Ultimately, life is not about us, but about him and his kingdom. Thus we are people who have been <u>sent</u>: sent to care and sent to preach. We are sent into a lost and hurting world to tell them about the God who made them uniquely and loves them dearly. We are sent to love extravagantly, to be his hands and his feet.

These two movements are pretty simple actually, but must always be practiced in the right order—*with* must always come before *sent*. In fact, *with* provides *sent* its direction and depth, its power and substance. But when we get it backwards, when we run to the world before running to our God, we soon find ourselves empty and barren, dry and burnt out…useless. Ministry must always depend on (and flow out of) our relationship with Jesus—rather than our relationship with Jesus depending on our ministry. So let us remember, this day and every day, to keep the first things first.

Respond:
Reflect on the phrases: *those he wanted*, and *that they might be with him*. Spend some time thinking about the fact that God wants you, and that he wants to be with you. How does this make you feel? What does it do *in* you? Now spend some time thinking about your mission. Where is he sending you? Who is he sending you to? How will you speak of him in your life and work today?

Rest:

Simply be with God for the next ten minutes. If your mind wanders, simply return to his presence with one of the phrases above: *I want you* or *I want to be with you.*

Seventeen

Read:

Then Jesus entered a house, and again a crowd gathered, so that he and his disciples were not even able to eat. When his family heard about this, they went to take charge of him, for they said, "He is out of his mind." And the teachers of the law who came down from Jerusalem said, "He is possessed by Beelzebub! By the prince of demons he is driving out demons." So Jesus called them and spoke to them in parables: "How can Satan drive out Satan? If a kingdom is divided against itself, that kingdom cannot stand. If a house is divided against itself, that house cannot stand. And if Satan opposes himself and is divided, he cannot stand; his end has come. In fact, no one can enter a strong man's house and carry off his possessions unless he first ties up the strong man. Then he can rob his house. I tell you the truth, all the sins and blasphemies of men will be forgiven them. But whoever blasphemes against the Holy Spirit will never be forgiven; he is guilty of an eternal sin." He said this because they were saying, "He has an evil spirit."

Then Jesus' mother and brothers arrived. Standing outside, they sent someone in to call him. A crowd was sitting around him, and they told him, "Your mother and brothers are outside looking for you." "Who are my mother and my brothers?" he asked. Then he looked at those seated in a circle around him and said, "Here are my mother and my brothers! Whoever does God's will is my brother and sister and mother." (Mark 3:20-35)

Reflect:

One of the Desert Fathers once said, *"A time is coming when men will go mad, and when they see someone who is not mad, they will attack him saying, 'You are mad, you are not like us.'"* This statement may have never been as true of anyone as it was of Jesus. He was so radically different—in both his thinking and his priorities—from the world and the culture around him. Therefore, he found himself in constant conflict with them. Even his own family joined in; they thought he was *out of his mind* and tried to *take charge of him* because of the things he said and the things he did.

And if that wasn't enough, the religious leaders were in conflict with him as well; even to the point of accusing him of being possessed. They had one problem after another with Jesus; until they eventually plotted to kill him because he was such a threat to their existence on every level. He threatened their power, their influence, and even their position in society. He also threatened their way of life, i.e., the way they practiced their faith. Jesus simply turned organized religion upside down, drawing a sharp contrast between what was true and genuine and lasting about faith with what he saw lived out in the lives of the Scribes and the Pharisees.

Jesus marched to the beat of a different drummer; to a different tune— the tune of the Spirit of God. While the Pharisees were all about being seen and getting noticed, Jesus was all about hidden places and the unseen roles. While the Pharisees were all about grasping for power and position and influence, Jesus was about emptying himself and total surrender to the will of the Father. While the Pharisees were all about pursuing status and prestige, Jesus was about pursuing the lost, the meek and the lowly; putting their needs before his own. And while the Pharisees were all about accumulating wealth and possessions, Jesus was about giving his very life away to redeem a broken and hurting world.

And it wasn't just what he did, it was also what he said that flew right in the face of the thinking and the attitude of the day. He was constantly saying things such as: *in order to save your life, you must lose your life,* and *the last will be first and the first will be last,* and *deny yourself and take up your cross and follow me.* Jesus seemed to value the things that were the direct opposite of everything the culture around him pursued and held as valuable.

And that is still the case today. If we truly seek to follow Jesus, it is going to put us at odds with the world around us –even the religious world. We will be so different and so radical that they are going to think we've lost our minds. They are going to think we've *gone mad* because we don't live the way that they live and don't love the things that they love.

They will be shocked that we value fruitfulness more than productivity, humility more than power, dependence more than independence, and compassion more than competition. They will be amazed that we are not concerned with accomplishment or popularity or accumulation of wealth. They will be dumbfounded that we are more concerned about doing God's will than doing our own. They will not be able to grasp that the real question of life for us is not, "*How does God fit into my life*?" but rather, "*How do I fit into God's plan and what is he doing in the world*?"

All this is flows from one major source: that Jesus is the point of existence, not us. Our very lives are all about Him, not about us. And our main task in this life is to give Him complete and total control of all that we do, think, and say. Now that is radical.

Respond:
Do you ever worry that people will think *you're out of your mind* because of your love and devotion to Jesus? What would make you begin to feel that way? How do you feel different from the world around you? How do you

feel too similar? What do you think God is saying to you (or calling you to) in this portion of Mark?

Rest:
Simply rest in Jesus for the next few minutes and in what he has spoken to you this day.

Eighteen

Read:
Again Jesus began to teach by the lake. The crowd that gathered around him was so large that he got into a boat and sat in it out on the lake, while all the people were along the shore at the water's edge. He taught them many things by parables, and in his teaching said: "Listen! A farmer went out to sow his seed. As he was scattering the seed, some fell along the path, and the birds came and ate it up. Some fell on rocky places, where it did not have much soil. It sprang up quickly, because the soil was shallow. But when the sun came up, the plants were scorched, and they withered because they had no root. Other seed fell among thorns, which grew up and choked the plants, so that they did not bear grain. Still other seed fell on good soil. It came up, grew and produced a crop, multiplying thirty, sixty, or even a hundred times." Then Jesus said, "He who has ears to hear, let him hear." When he was alone, the Twelve and the others around him asked him about the parables. He told them, "The secret of the kingdom of God has been given to you. But to those on the outside everything is said in parables so that, " 'they may be ever seeing but never perceiving, and ever hearing but never understanding; otherwise they might turn and be forgiven!' " Then Jesus said to them, "Don't you understand this parable? How then will you understand any parable? The farmer sows the word. Some people are like seed along the path, where the word is sown. As soon as they hear it, Satan comes and takes away the word that was sown in them. Others, like seed sown on rocky places, hear the word and at once receive it with joy. But since they have no root, they last only a short time. When trouble or persecution comes because of the word, they quickly fall away. Still others, like seed sown among thorns, hear the word; but the worries of this life, the deceitfulness of wealth and the desires for other things come in and choke the word, making it unfruitful. Others, like seed sown on good soil, hear the word, accept it, and produce a crop—thirty, sixty or even a hundred times what was sown." (Mark 4:1-20)

Reflect:
Metaphor is the language of the kingdom. It uses physical objects to teach us deep spiritual truths. Time after time Jesus uses metaphor to help

explain the mysteries of God. This familiar parable is no exception; it is chocked full of pictures of what life with God *is really like*.

For instance, it shows us that God's Word is like seed—filled with life and possibility. As it is scattered and falls in the right sort of soil, it is able to come to life and grow and bear much fruit. Therefore, if we desire to be filled with the life and fruit of the Spirit, we must be constantly planting the Word within our hearts and allowing it space and time and soil to grow and take root and produce. Where is the Word growing within you during this season?

The parable also tells us that our soul is like soil—it must be receptive and fertile in order to allow the seed of the Word to be as fruitful as possible. If our soul is hardened, or filled with rocks and/or thorns, it will eventually keep the planted Word from being fruitful within us. Therefore, a particular amount of gardening, or soul tending, is necessary for the conditions to be right for long-term growth. What is the current state of your heart and soul? Where are your hardened places? Where are the rocks and thorns within you that are obstacles to growth and fruitfulness? And where does your soul seem fertile and ready and fruitful?

One other truth the parable reveals to us is that ministry is a lot like farming. It is hard, slow work. It does not feel very heroic and involves a lot of difficult and mundane tasks. It involves knowing your land well—constantly walking the fields to check their condition and to stay attentive to what needs to be done (and when). It is work that's messy and will get your hands dirty. There is no way to do it from a distance—you have to be in it up to your elbows. It is not just a hobby, but an entire way of life (a calling). It is a life filled with tilling the soil, and weeding, and digging. It is a life filled with plowing up the hard ground and breaking up the rocky soil. It is a life filled with doing whatever it takes to make the soil (soul) as receptive as possible to the seed of the Word. Where in your life do you feel like you are a farmer working in the field; or scattering seed; or reaping a harvest?

It is completely amazing that all of this truth (and more) comes from one simple story—with so many different levels of understanding and so many different points of entry. It is a story to step inside of and learn the mysteries of God, as well as the mysteries of our own hearts and lives. What does this parable say to you? What word or image seems the most relevant to your life? What part of the picture speaks most clearly to your current story?

Respond:
Prayerfully reflect on the following questions and write about them (or draw a picture of your "field") in your journal: What is the condition of your soil (soul)? Where are you hardened? Where are you rocky? Where are there thorns? What work needs to take place within you to make your soil receptive?

Ask God to do that work. Ask Him to show you how to make your soul more receptive. Where is the Word bringing up life within you? Where is there growth? Where is there fruit? Thank God for it and ask Him to enable it to continue.

Rest:
Just be with God for the next few minutes. Be who and what you are (thorns and all), knowing that He is the one who will bring about the fruit—it is nothing we can produce or manufacture. Simply rest in His care.

Nineteen

Read:
He said to them, "Do you bring in a lamp to put it under a bowl or a bed? Instead, don't you put it on its stand? For whatever is hidden is meant to be disclosed, and whatever is concealed is meant to be brought out into the open. If anyone has ears to hear, let him hear."   "Consider carefully what you hear," he continued. "With the measure you use, it will be measured to you—and even more. Whoever has will be given more; whoever does not have, even what he has will be taken from him." (Mark 4:21-25)

Reflect:
If anyone has ears, let him hear. Consider carefully what you hear. It is hard to exaggerate the importance of these words in the spiritual life. They are so vital; such an integral part of life with God. Yet a part we don't practice easily or often. Why is that?

Possibly it is because the practice of hearing God involves a lot more than just listening to his words. It involves actually hearing (considering carefully) what he is saying *to us*. It is so easy to get those two things confused. Sometimes we can listen to what someone is saying to us generally, but still fail to hear what they are saying *to us* specifically. And this specific-type of hearing is by far the most personal and transformational type.

It is the difference between hearing informationally (simply taking in information) and hearing formationally (hearing in a way that forms and transforms us). It is the difference between religion and relationship, between dry ritual and life-changing encounter. In order to grow in our intimacy with Jesus, we must begin to practice the art of listening not just to the words, but beneath the words—to somehow be able to taste and savor them; to chew on and reflect on them. It involves what Eugene Peterson once called *turning our eyes into ears*. Or what others have referred to as *listening with the ear of our hearts*. And when we are able to listen in this way, maybe we will be able to truly hear his voice…and just maybe that voice will change us forever.

Respond:
Listen for God's voice in his Word today. Read the passage again and again. What word or image seems to capture your attention? Why? Reflect on it. Chew on it. Savor the flavor of it. Listen for his voice in it. Try to hear him. What do you think God is saying to you?

Rest:
Spend a few minutes just enjoying whatever it is you received from God this day (even if it was his silence), knowing that this is his gift to you.

Twenty

Read:
He also said, "This is what the kingdom of God is like. A man scatters seed on the ground. Night and day, whether he sleeps or gets up, the seed sprouts and grows, though he does not know how. All by itself the soil produces grain—first the stalk, then the head, then the full kernel in the head. As soon as the grain is ripe, he puts the sickle to it, because the harvest has come." (Mark 4:26-29)

Reflect:
What would it be like to be a seed? What does a seed's life involve? Does a seed have to agree to anything, other than to be just what it is? Does a seed have to say *yes* to being what it is? Or is a seed a *yes*? Does it know what it is to become? And when? Or does it just happen?

Does it have to strain or try? Does it take effort? What would it be like to be filled with such possibility, and life, and new birth? What would it be like to contain mystery within? What would it be like if your entire job was just to *be*; and the rest was simply a result of that?

And what about you? Is there a seed growing within you this day?

Respond:
What seed has been planted within you by God recently; and how is it growing and taking shape? Reflect on that question and write about it (or draw a picture of it) in your journal.

Rest:
Simply rest in Him for a few minutes, knowing that the work is His…He will do it.

Twenty-One

Read:
Again he said, "What shall we say the kingdom of God is like, or what parable shall we use to describe it? It is like a mustard seed, which is the smallest seed you plant in the ground. Yet when planted, it grows and becomes the largest of all garden plants, with such big branches that the birds of the air can perch in its shade." With many similar parables Jesus spoke the word to them, as much as they could understand. He did not say anything to them without using a parable. But when he was alone with his own disciples, he explained everything. (Mark 4:30-34)

Reflect:

watering the seed
and watching
and believing
and hoping
and waiting
for it to grow
    and emerge from the soil
so it can be seen
what sort of thing is this that grows within?
    in the deep rich darkness
    that is not dark to you
knowing that there is growth within
but not knowing quite what it is
knowing and not knowing
trusting the seed to do its job
it knows what it is to become
and when
and so i water
and watch
and believe
and hope
and wait
and know
and not know

Respond:
Sometimes the largest and most significant works of God within us remain hidden for a long time before we are able to see, identify, and name them. And quite often they will start out from tiny, almost indiscernible beginnings. Therefore we must pay careful attention to all that is going on around us and within us. Walk the soil of your soul today looking for signs of life. Be very attentive to anything and everything that seems to be

growing within you during this season. What do you see? What growth can you identify and name? What is still unseen? What do you think is going on beneath the soil of your soul right now?

Rest:
Today (as you did yesterday) rest in the knowledge that God is at work, even if the fruit of that work is not yet visible to you. Trust that one day it will be. In fact, one day it will grow into *the largest of all garden plants.*

Twenty-Two

Read:
That day when evening came, he said to his disciples, "Let us go over to the other side." Leaving the crowd behind, they took him along, just as he was, in the boat. There were also other boats with him. A furious squall came up, and the waves broke over the boat, so that it was nearly swamped. Jesus was in the stern, sleeping on a cushion. The disciples woke him and said to him, "Teacher, don't you care if we drown?" He got up, rebuked the wind and said to the waves, "Quiet! Be still!" Then the wind died down and it was completely calm. He said to his disciples, "Why are you so afraid? Do you still have no faith?" They were terrified and asked each other, "Who is this? Even the wind and the waves obey him!" (Mark 4:35-41)

Reflect:
Life is so fragile at times. One minute the skies are blue, the sun is shining, and all is well with the world. And the next, all hell seems to break loose—storms, waves, chaos, frenzy, pain, suffering—just hanging on for dear life. Trying desperately to survive or stay afloat.

And when the *furious squall* comes, the questions of our heart seem more numerous that the waves on the sea. What in the world is going on? Why is this happening? Why me?

So, in our desperation, we turn to God. Where are you? Are you asleep? Don't you care if we drown? All of these are gut-wrenchingly honest questions; raw and real. They are questions that we desperately need to have answered. Questions that show us what the foundation of our lives really rests upon. Questions that ultimately show us—for better or worse—what our faith is really made of.

And they are questions that, depending on where we go with them and how they are answered, will determine what we truly believe about life and faith and God. Are we on our own? Do we have to fend for ourselves? Or is there really a God who cares? Is there really a God who can help us make sense out of all this? Is there really a God that can bring *calm* into the midst of chaos?

What we find, if and when we turn to Jesus in the midst of our storms, is that he indeed is always true to his name—Immanuel—God with us. He indeed is present—and not asleep. He indeed cares for us deeply, in ways that we could never imagine.

What we find out is that he indeed is able to bring *calm* into the midst of chaos; peace into the midst of upheaval. He, indeed, is God and he, indeed, can be trusted—even in the midst of the storms. Even when we feel like we are about to go down, about to drown, about to be swamped. He indeed, can *rebuke the wind and the waves*. He indeed, can utter the words *Quiet! Be still!* And he indeed, can make the *wind die down* and the sea become *completely calm*. Turn to him and see for yourself.

Respond:
What is life like for you right now? What do your seas look like? Draw a picture of them in your journal. Are there storms in your life right now? Where do you turn in the midst of them? What are the questions of your heart? Bring it all to Jesus this day and ask for his presence and his peace.

Rest:
Take five minutes to be still before God. Repeat the words, "*Quiet! Be still!*" slowly and quietly, over and over again, in an attempt to allow him to calm the waters of your soul.

Twenty-Three

Read:
They went across the lake to the region of the Gerasenes. When Jesus got out of the boat, a man with an evil spirit came from the tombs to meet him. This man lived in the tombs, and no one could bind him any more, not even with a chain. For he had often been chained hand and foot, but he tore the chains apart and broke the irons on his feet. No one was strong enough to subdue him. Night and day among the tombs and in the hills he would cry out and cut himself with stones.

When he saw Jesus from a distance, he ran and fell on his knees in front of him. He shouted at the top of his voice, "What do you want with me, Jesus, Son of the Most High God? Swear to God that you won't torture me!" For Jesus had said to him, "Come out of this man, you evil spirit!"

Then Jesus asked him, "What is your name?"

"My name is Legion," he replied, "for we are many."

And he begged Jesus again and again not to send them out of the area.

A large herd of pigs was feeding on the nearby hillside. The demons begged Jesus, "Send us among the pigs; allow us to go into them." He gave them permission, and the evil spirits came out and went into the pigs.

The herd, about two thousand in number, rushed down the steep bank into the lake and were drowned.

Those tending the pigs ran off and reported this in the town and countryside, and the people went out to see what had happened. When they came to Jesus, they saw the man who had been possessed by the legion of demons, sitting there, dressed and in his right mind; and they were afraid. Those who had seen it told the people what had happened to the demon-possessed man—and told about the pigs as well. Then the people began to plead with Jesus to leave their region.

As Jesus was getting into the boat, the man who had been demon-possessed begged to go with him. Jesus did not let him, but said, "Go home to your family and tell them how much the Lord has done for you, and how he has had mercy on you." So the man went away and began to tell in the Decapolis how much Jesus had done for him. And all the people were amazed. (Mark 5:1-20)

Reflect:
"What is your name?" On the surface it appears to be an easy enough question; relatively harmless it would seem. But at the same time, it is a question that is so profound. Because a name can tell us something significant about a person's identity, about who they really are, about who they really believe themselves to be. Which makes Jesus' question to the tortured soul a telling one: *Who are you? Who do you believe yourself to be?*

It's an important question. A question we all must struggle to try and answer. Who am I, really? How will I attempt to define myself? What will give me a true sense of identity? What am I counting on to give me worth or value?

Most of us work our whole lives to find answers to these questions—to make a name for ourselves. The problem is that the name we make for ourselves will never be our true name. Because our true identity can never be achieved, it must always be bestowed. And it can only be bestowed by the One who made us.

My name is Legion, the man answers, *for we are many.* In other words *I have no idea who I am. There are so many different people (voices) in here it is impossible to tell.* That is his current reality. That is the basis from which he is living his life. We all tend to live out of the name we most believe to be true about us.

His name was *Legion*. A legion was believed to be around 5,000 soldiers, so obviously bearing that name meant that this man was a mass of chaos and confusion within. He was everybody. And because he was everybody, he was really nobody at all. That is undoubtedly the way he must have felt: insignificant, worthless, unlovable...a nobody. He was destined for a life of confusion, despair, and loneliness.

That is the situation Jesus steps into in Gerasa with this man who spent his life in the tombs, cutting himself with stones, breaking chains, and crying out for some sort of relief from his torment. And while everyone else is running away from him, Jesus runs toward him, meeting him right where he is; in the middle of his brokenness and pain. And in the process somehow *Legion* receives a brand new name and, therefore, a brand new life. And he is completely and totally transformed.

Respond:
Spend some time this morning asking God to show you his real name for you—the one that is most truly a reflection of who He created you to be. Read Revelation 2:17. What name do you think is written on your white stone?

Rest:
Simply rest in the name that God has spoken to you. Your value and worth are dependent completely on him—you no longer have to prove yourself to anyone.

Twenty-Four

Read:
When Jesus had again crossed over by boat to the other side of the lake, a large crowd gathered around him while he was by the lake. Then one of the synagogue rulers, named Jairus, came there. Seeing Jesus, he fell at his feet and pleaded earnestly with him, "My little daughter is dying. Please come and put your hands on her so that she will be healed and live." So Jesus went with him.

A large crowd followed and pressed around him. And a woman was there who had been subject to bleeding for twelve years. She had suffered a great deal under the care of many doctors and had spent all she had, yet instead of getting better she grew worse. When she heard about Jesus, she came up behind him in the crowd and touched his cloak, because she thought, "If I just touch his clothes, I will be healed." Immediately her bleeding stopped and she felt in her body that she was freed from her suffering.

At once Jesus realized that power had gone out from him. He turned around in the crowd and asked, "Who touched my clothes?"

"You see the people crowding against you," his disciples answered, "and yet you can ask, 'Who touched me?' "

But Jesus kept looking around to see who had done it.

Then the woman, knowing what had happened to her, came and fell at his feet and, trembling with fear, told him the whole truth. He said to her, "Daughter, your faith has healed you. Go in peace and be freed from your suffering." (Mark 5:21-34)

Reflect:
something has gone terribly wrong.
a long slow *bleeding* deep within
has been her constant companion
for as long as she can remember.
so many things, she has tried
to make the bleeding stop,
or at least to make her feel better
if even for a moment.
but the long line of solutions have failed her,
so here she stands
even worse off than she was before.
desperately *grasping* for wholeness, or healing,
or even a glimmer of hope.

maybe Jesus…
maybe He will…
be able to stop the bleeding of her weary heart.

"if only I can get near enough to reach out and touch"
and when she finally grasps for him
the bleeding stops, the wound is healed
the broken is made whole.
relief streaks down her tearstained cheeks
freedom…finally.

he turns and looks, his gaze upon her.
she falls to her knees in fear and confusion.
he kneels down, his hand gently lifting her chin
in order to see her face.
he looks deeply into her eyes.

"daughter" he tenderly whispers…
to the depths of her heart and soul.
"you are mine."
indescribable intimacy and care
in the middle of a crowded street.

"your faith has healed you. go in peace"
with a gentle smile upon his lips,
knowing that this is what she most deeply longs for.

"be freed from your suffering"
and indeed she is.
no more bleeding, no more grasping,
only love.

and in the midst of her bleeding,
and her grasping, and her healing
i am reminded of my need for the same.
reminded of the open wound of my insecurity,
of my grasping for value and affection...
when only One offers the touch
that will bring wholeness and freedom
and life

Respond:

In what ways do you feel like you are bleeding inside? What is the source of this bleeding? In what ways has your bleeding heart caused you to grasp? What are you grasping for? Reflect on these questions and write about them in your journal.

What would it mean for Jesus to touch this wounded, bleeding place and make it whole again? How does truly believing you are His daughter/son speak into this bleeding and grasping?

Rest:

Hear His words to you this day and find rest in them: *"Daughter/Son, your faith has healed you. Go in peace and be freed from your suffering."*

Twenty-Five

Read:

While Jesus was still speaking, some men came from the house of Jairus, the synagogue ruler. "Your daughter is dead," they said. "Why bother the teacher anymore?" Ignoring what they said, Jesus told the synagogue ruler, "Don't be afraid; just believe."

He did not let anyone follow him except Peter, James and John the brother of James. When they came to the home of the synagogue ruler, Jesus saw a commotion, with people crying and wailing loudly. He went in and said to them, "Why all this commotion and wailing? The child is not dead but asleep." But they laughed at him.

After he put them all out, he took the child's father and mother and the disciples who were with him, and went in where the child was. He took her by the hand and said to her, "Talitha koum!" (which means, "Little girl, I say to you, get up!"). Immediately the girl stood up and walked around (she was twelve years old). At this they were completely astonished. He gave strict orders not to let anyone know about this, and told them to give her something to eat. (Mark 5:35-43)

Reflect:

One had been bleeding for twelve years; the other was just twelve years old. One had probably seen a good bit of her life come and go; the other seemingly had her whole life ahead of her. One was from a prominent family; the other was just a face in the crowd. One had a loving father that would go to any length to give his little girl every opportunity available to be healed; the other had most likely been abandoned by her family long ago because of her lengthy bout with an illness that rendered her ceremonially unclean—untouchable.

But while there were significant differences between the two, there were also many similarities. For both, life had taken a terribly wrong turn. Both had grasped for healing and wholeness from every available avenue. Both were now at the end of their rope—needy and desperate. Both had some sense that Jesus was their final real hope. And most importantly, though they had yet to realize it, both were dearly loved daughters of God.

After meeting one in the midst of a crowded street, Jesus now turns in the direction of the other. But it appears that, for this little one, he is too late. Jesus enters the house, taking a small group of family and friends with him. He goes into the room where the little girl is lying. He bends over, gently taking her hand, and whispers tenderly in her ear, "*Little girl, get up.*" Or literally, in Aramaic, *"Little Lamb, Arise!"* His *little lamb* opens her eyes and gets up from her bed, as if simply waking from a peaceful night's sleep.

Desperation turns to celebration; mourning to dancing. The small band of onlookers is both amazed and overjoyed. Jesus turns to Jairus and his wife and, with a soft smile on his lips, says, with a wink, "Now… why don't you give her something to eat."

Respond:

Which of the two stories do you feel most a part of? Which most speaks to the state of your life and heart at the moment? Put yourself in that particular story. What are you feeling? What are you thinking? Where do you most need healing? What are your deepest longings? Where do you yearn to hear the words of Jesus speaking to your heart?

Which words resonate most within you right now? *"Daughter/Son, your faith has healed you. Go in peace and be freed from your suffering."* Or "*Little lamb, Arise!*"

Rest:

Rest in the gentle, healing touch of your Creator.

Twenty-Six

Read:

Jesus left there and went to his hometown, accompanied by his disciples. When the Sabbath came, he began to teach in the synagogue, and many who heard him were amazed.

"Where did this man get these things?" they asked. "What's this wisdom that has been given him, that he even does miracles! Isn't this the carpenter? Isn't this Mary's son and the brother of James, Joseph, Judas and Simon? Aren't his sisters here with us?" And they took offense at him.

Jesus said to them, "Only in his hometown, among his relatives and in his own house is a prophet without honor." He could not do any miracles there, except lay his hands on a few sick people and heal them. And he was amazed at their lack of faith. (Mark 6:1-6)

Reflect:

It seems like the hardest place on earth to live a transformed life is in our own families, and our own *hometowns*. Have you ever wondered why that is? Have you ever reflected on what the dynamics and forces are that make it that way? In fact wouldn't you think that just the opposite should be true? Jesus surely seemed to be well acquainted with this phenomenon.

It is so interesting how *home* always tries to keep us in our place, to keep us in the same mold in which we grew up. It's a kind of gravitational pull that seems to resist change and transformation at all costs. In technical terms it's called homeostasis which comes from the Greek words, *homoios*, meaning "of the same kind" and *stasis*, meaning "standing still." Thus, homeostasis is the tendency of a system to resist change in order to maintain its current state or order, no matter how dysfunctional that state or order may be.

It's even more interesting that even Jesus' *home* tried to exert this pressure on him. It tried to define who he was and who he could (and could not) become. Thankfully Jesus refused to comply. He didn't succumb to the pressures *home* can exert on us to try and keep us in a particular place and role. His words and actions give us hope that it does not have to be this way—we can rise above the pressures that our homes and our hometowns exert on us to try and keep us "in our place." We can resist the homeostatic forces and live transformed lives even in the midst of our family systems.

Respond:

Draw a picture of the family you grew up in. Now look closely at your picture and see what it tells you about the family system. What were the dynamics between family members? What was each person's place or role within the family? What was yours? In what ways do you still have trouble breaking out of those patterns or roles? In what ways do you have trouble living a transformed life in the middle of your family?

Rest:
Rest in the freedom that Jesus offers you from your old habits, patterns, and roles. Repeat the prayer: "I belong to You, O God." And allow the truth of that prayer to descend from your mind into your heart and take root within you.

Twenty-Seven

Read:
Then Jesus went around teaching from village to village. Calling the Twelve to him, he sent them out two by two and gave them authority over evil spirits.

These were his instructions: "Take nothing for the journey except a staff—no bread, no bag, no money in your belts. Wear sandals but not an extra tunic. Whenever you enter a house, stay there until you leave that town. And if any place will not welcome you or listen to you, shake the dust off your feet when you leave, as a testimony against them."

They went out and preached that people should repent. They drove out many demons and anointed many sick people with oil and healed them. (Mark 6:6-13)

Reflect:
Jesus was so purposeful and so intentional in all that he did—especially with his disciples. When it came to those closest to him he was always trying to open their eyes to who he really was and what he was really about. It seems like he was always teaching them; always training, always molding. Obviously he knew that when his time came to leave this world that they must be ready to take up the mission.

And so, in this instance, he calls them together for some instructions. He bestows upon them his power and his authority, and then sends them out for a trial run. He sends them two-by-two to show them the necessity of community in mission. Mission is never best done alone; there is strength in numbers. Or as Ecclesiastes puts it, "Two are better than one."

He tells them what not to take with them on the journey, in order to help them learn to trust God's resources rather than their own. He tells them that when they enter a house, to stay there; which helps them understand the value of relationship in ministry. Mission is never a hit and run proposition. God is a God of relationship and the message of the gospel is meant to be shared in the context of those relationships.

And so they go out, and they preach, and they heal, and they care, and they learn. And people are impacted, they repent—they turn back toward

God. And people are healed—made whole once again. And the disciples begin to see a picture (unbeknownst to them) of what life will look like when Jesus is with them in Spirit, but no longer in body.

Respond:

Where do you think God could be sending you with his gospel? Ask him who the people are that he wants you to go to. Read his instructions to the disciples again and write down what those instructions mean for you as you go.

Rest:

Place your ministry completely in God's hands and trust that He will work in the lives of those He is sending you to. It is His work, rest in His power, provision, and care.

Twenty-Eight

Read:

King Herod heard about this, for Jesus' name had become well known. Some were saying, "John the Baptist has been raised from the dead, and that is why miraculous powers are at work in him."

Others said, "He is Elijah."

And still others claimed, "He is a prophet, like one of the prophets of long ago."

But when Herod heard this, he said, "John, the man I beheaded, has been raised from the dead!"

For Herod himself had given orders to have John arrested, and he had him bound and put in prison. He did this because of Herodias, his brother Philip's wife, whom he had married. For John had been saying to Herod, "It is not lawful for you to have your brother's wife." So Herodias nursed a grudge against John and wanted to kill him. But she was not able to, because Herod feared John and protected him, knowing him to be a righteous and holy man. When Herod heard John, he was greatly puzzled; yet he liked to listen to him.

Finally the opportune time came. On his birthday Herod gave a banquet for his high officials and military commanders and the leading men of Galilee. When the daughter of Herodias came in and danced, she pleased Herod and his dinner guests.

The king said to the girl, "Ask me for anything you want, and I'll give it to you." And he promised her with an oath, "Whatever you ask I will give you, up to half my kingdom."

She went out and said to her mother, "What shall I ask for?"

"The head of John the Baptist," she answered.

At once the girl hurried in to the king with the request: "I want you to give me right now the head of John the Baptist on a platter."

The king was greatly distressed, but because of his oaths and his dinner guests, he did not want to refuse her. So he immediately sent an executioner with orders to bring John's head. The man went, beheaded John in the prison, and brought back his head on a platter. He presented it to the girl, and she gave it to her mother. On hearing of this, John's disciples came and took his body and laid it in a tomb. (Mark 6:14-29)

Reflect:
There's no way around it. Life with God is costly. In fact, for those who truly desire to follow Jesus it costs them everything—even their lives. John the Baptist was one of many to find this out. I wonder if he ever realized it would probably turn out this way? And if he did, how did he feel about that?

He was obviously willing, since throughout his entire adult life he had been known as "that guy." That guy that gave up his own will to do the will of God—living in the desert, wearing the strange clothes, eating a strange diet; passionate about the message of the coming Messiah. He was a man on a mission, and his mission was far more important to him than his life.

We are not John the Baptist, and we do not live in the days in which he lived, but what about us? What does this all mean for you and me? What does our decision to follow Jesus really cost us? And in what ways are we called to give up our lives for the sake of Christ? What does that look like on a daily basis? It is a theme that will be recurring as we go along, so if you don't have answers now, don't worry, He will come back to it.

Respond:
As you think about the life and the sacrifice of John the Baptist, spend some time thinking about what God might be asking you to sacrifice for His kingdom. In what ways (or with what people) is God asking you to take a risk and venture out of your comfort zone in an effort to take His message to those in your life and world?

Rest:
Place your life, this day, in the eternal hands of our God, who is bigger than fear and death—and able to keep you until the day of Christ Jesus.

Twenty-Nine

Read:
The apostles gathered around Jesus and reported to him all they had done and taught. Then, because so many people were coming and going

that they did not even have a chance to eat, he said to them, "Come with me by yourselves to a quiet place and get some rest."

So they went away by themselves in a boat to a solitary place. But many who saw them leaving recognized them and ran on foot from all the towns and got there ahead of them. When Jesus landed and saw a large crowd, he had compassion on them, because they were like sheep without a shepherd. So he began teaching them many things.

By this time it was late in the day, so his disciples came to him. "This is a remote place," they said, "and it's already very late. Send the people away so they can go to the surrounding countryside and villages and buy themselves something to eat."

But he answered, "You give them something to eat."

They said to him, "That would take eight months of a man's wages! Are we to go and spend that much on bread and give it to them to eat?"

"How many loaves do you have?" he asked. "Go and see."

When they found out, they said, "Five—and two fish."

Then Jesus directed them to have all the people sit down in groups on the green grass. So they sat down in groups of hundreds and fifties. Taking the five loaves and the two fish and looking up to heaven, he gave thanks and broke the loaves. Then he gave them to his disciples to set before the people. He also divided the two fish among them all. They all ate and were satisfied, and the disciples picked up twelve basketfuls of broken pieces of bread and fish. The number of the men who had eaten was five thousand. (Mark 6:30-44)

Reflect:
I love it. Jesus could have done it so many different ways and could've said so many different things, but this is what he said to them. *You give them something to eat.* Was he giving them a preview of what it would be like when He was no longer around? Or was He trying to help them learn the painful truth that apart from Him we have absolutely nothing to give? Whatever the case, it was brilliant…and it had them scrambling.

How many loaves do you have? Five? And two fish? Have everyone sit down in groups in the grass. And the disciples did as they were told. What in the world was about to happen? What could Jesus possibly do with such a pittance?

He took the loaves and fish, blessed it, and gave each disciple a portion to take to the people. So the disciples went out among the crowd wondering how far the little bit they had received could possibly last in a crowd so large. And as they began to pass out the food, it kept going. Where was it all coming from?

And everyone ate…and ate…until they all were satisfied—all 5,000-10,000 people! Absolutely amazing! And if that weren't enough, as they went out to collect the leftovers, they picked up twelve baskets full of food—one for each of them. Who should be surprised?

But there is one thing I have always wondered about this scene. When the disciples were passing out the food, where was Jesus? Was He with them passing out loaves and fish as well? Did he decide to sit in one of the groups and join them for a satisfying meal and some great conversation? Was he walking around caring for each of the twelve disciples as they carried out his directions? Was he off by himself praying? Or was he simply standing in the midst of it all with a big smile on his face enjoying every moment of what was unfolding around him? No one can know for sure, and I think I'm glad of that. It leaves something to our imaginations. And by doing so it lets us know a little bit more about what each of us really believes God to be like.

Respond:
Scan the horizon of the scene just described, looking for Jesus. Where is he in this picture? Where do you most believe he would have been? Why? What does it tell you about what you really believe to be true about Jesus?

Rest:
Simply rest in the spiritual food God has fed you with this day. Sit and savor the feeling of having been fed much and fed well; the way you might feel with friends around the table after of terrific meal together. Make sure to thank Him for His provision.

Thirty

Read:
Immediately Jesus made his disciples get into the boat and go on ahead of him to Bethsaida, while he dismissed the crowd. After leaving them, he went up on a mountainside to pray.

When evening came, the boat was in the middle of the lake, and he was alone on land. He saw the disciples straining at the oars, because the wind was against them. About the fourth watch of the night he went out to them, walking on the lake. He was about to pass by them, but when they saw him walking on the lake, they thought he was a ghost. They cried out, because they all saw him and were terrified.

Immediately he spoke to them and said, "Take courage! It is I. Don't be afraid." Then he climbed into the boat with them, and the wind died down. They were completely amazed, for they had not understood about the loaves; their hearts were hardened. (Mark 6:45-52)

Reflect:
The older I get, the more I realize that quite possibly the biggest single enemy of our spiritual lives (other than Satan himself) is fear. Fear seems

to be at the very core of all the things that battle against my heart and soul. At the core of my busyness is fear. At the core of my insecurity is fear. At the core of my anxiety is fear. At the core of my competitiveness...you guessed it—fear. Fear of not having what it takes. Fear of not having any value. Fear of not being lovable. The list goes on and on.

And maybe the main reason this enemy is so strong and dangerous is that by and large it is a hidden enemy. We never really look beneath the surface of our more familiar enemies to spot it. We rarely follow any of these foes down far enough to see what is at their root. And when we don't know what we are really fighting, how can we possibly be victorious? We just keep getting defeated over and over again. This fear robs us of the intimacy we were created for. It robs us of the freedom that God longs for us to enjoy. It robs us of genuinely loving relationships. It simply controls the way we live our lives.

What are we to do? How can we possibly fight against this? A first step would seem to be identifying and *naming* our fears. Somehow naming our fears takes some of their power away to control us. Ann Lamott once said, "When you make friends with fear, it can't rule you." Once our enemy is identified it makes it much easier to wage war.

Secondly, we need to remember that our real enemy (Satan) is the "father of lies." He will use his lies to manipulate us into believing whatever he can. Because of this, it seems that we need to ask ourselves, "What lies are we believing that are simply not true? How is our seeing or thinking distorted?" When the disciples were on the sea battling against the storm (Mark 6:45-52) they screamed out in terror because they thought Jesus was a ghost. Now it wasn't really a ghost upon the water... they just thought it was. It was their distorted thinking and seeing that gave power to their fears. Once they saw things clearly and therefore thought about things more accurately—they were able to put everything in perspective.

Which brings us to the biggest weapon we have been given to wage war against fear—and that is what John calls "perfect love" (1 John 4:18). It is perfect love that puts everything in perspective for us. Once the voice of perfect love calls out to us, "Take courage. It is I. Don't be afraid." Then we are reminded that the love of the one who made us, and called us into being, and cares for us more than we can even care for ourselves, is in control of all things. And His heart for us is good—he can be trusted even when circumstances look dire because he loves us so immensely and completely. When he speaks His words of affection and peace and we hear and truly believe them; then we know that if he is with us—it will be well. Whatever it is, whatever the seas look like, it will be well.

Respond:
Spend some time reflecting on and naming your deepest fears. Write them down in your journal. How do these fears most often manifest themselves in your life? What would it look like to live a life controlled by love and not by fear in these areas?

Rest:
Rest in His words to you this day: *"Take courage. It is I. Don't be afraid."*
Repeat those words over and over until they take root in your heart.

Thirty-One

Read:
When they had crossed over, they landed at Gennesaret and anchored there. As soon as they got out of the boat, people recognized Jesus. They ran throughout that whole region and carried the sick on mats to wherever they heard he was. And wherever he went—into villages, towns or countryside—they placed the sick in the marketplaces. They begged him to let them touch even the edge of his cloak, and all who touched him were healed. (Mark 6:53-56)

Reflect:
People were just drawn to Jesus. We see it throughout Mark's entire gospel. Crowds pressed against him in the streets, whole towns gathered at his door, thousands followed him to a *remote place* just to hear his words. No length was too far to go to; they went around lakes, they dug holes in roofs, and they climbed sycamore trees.

And in this case, they ran. *They ran throughout that whole region and carried the sick on mats to wherever they heard he was.* What was it about Jesus that made people run toward him? And what is it about us, these days, that makes us believe people wouldn't do the same now?

It seems that most of us think that if Jesus just showed up one day—at our job, or in our neighborhood, or at our school, or maybe even in our churches—that people would do something other than run to meet him. Most might imagine that people would either run the other direction or ignore him completely. Why do we believe that?

Could it be that we've simply lost track of who Jesus really is? Could it be that we have forgotten how much the lost and the lonely, the broken and the needy, the fearful and the insecure, were drawn to Jesus. And all of us, if we willing to admit it, are at least one of those things all the time—no matter how we might try to cover it up or make it look like we've got it all together. When we are truly able to stare our own brokenness in the face, then we will be like the folks of Gennesaret; running to see Jesus, the only one who can touch our broken lives and make them whole again.

Respond:
Where are you most in need of God's healing touch? Hold that place before Him in prayer. Ask Him to touch you and make you whole in that

area. Now pray for others in your life and world that are deeply in need of the healing touch of Jesus as well.

Rest:
Rest in the fact that the healing touch of Jesus is upon you at this very moment. Feel the gentle warmth of His hand as He brings healing and wholeness to your broken and vulnerable places.

Thirty-Two

Read:
The Pharisees and some of the teachers of the law who had come from Jerusalem gathered around Jesus and saw some of his disciples eating food with hands that were "unclean," that is, unwashed. (The Pharisees and all the Jews do not eat unless they give their hands a ceremonial washing, holding to the tradition of the elders. When they come from the marketplace they do not eat unless they wash. And they observe many other traditions, such as the washing of cups, pitchers and kettles.)

So the Pharisees and teachers of the law asked Jesus, "Why don't your disciples live according to the tradition of the elders instead of eating their food with 'unclean' hands?"

He replied, "Isaiah was right when he prophesied about you hypocrites; as it is written:

" 'These people honor me with their lips, but their hearts are far from me. They worship me in vain; their teachings are but rules taught by men." You have let go of the commands of God and are holding on to the traditions of men."

And he said to them: "You have a fine way of setting aside the commands of God in order to observe your own traditions! For Moses said, 'Honor your father and your mother,' and, 'Anyone who curses his father or mother must be put to death.' But you say that if a man says to his father or mother: 'Whatever help you might otherwise have received from me is Corban' (that is, a gift devoted to God), then you no longer let him do anything for his father or mother. Thus you nullify the word of God by your tradition that you have handed down. And you do many things like that."

Again Jesus called the crowd to him and said, "Listen to me, everyone, and understand this. Nothing outside a man can make him 'unclean' by going into him. Rather, it is what comes out of a man that makes him 'unclean.' "

After he had left the crowd and entered the house, his disciples asked him about this parable. "Are you so dull?" he asked. "Don't you see that nothing that enters a man from the outside can make him 'unclean'? For it doesn't go into his heart but into his stomach, and then out of his body." (In saying this, Jesus declared all foods "clean.")

He went on: "What comes out of a man is what makes him 'unclean.' For from within, out of men's hearts, come evil thoughts, sexual immorality, theft, murder, adultery, greed, malice, deceit, lewdness, envy, slander, arrogance and folly. All these evils come from inside and make a man 'unclean.' " (Mark 7:1-23)

Reflect:
The heart is the center of life. It is that place within us at which exists our deepest core. It is that part of us where our affections reside; as well as the source from which they arise. And our affections determine so much about us.

Jesus knew this very well. He knew that there is a direct link between our hearts and our lives; between who, or what, we love and how we live. It is simply how we were made. Jesus knew that if you want to see what someone truly loves, all you have to do is take a look at how they live and it will give you a pretty good indication. Because when you truly love someone, it always shows; you will desire to please them in any and every way possible. The love you have for them will determine everything.

It is our hearts that make us who we really are, so ultimately, it is our hearts that God really wants, not just our behavior. For God knows full well that when he fully has our hearts, our behavior will always follow. Thus the heart is the source of life—the wellspring of all our thoughts, actions, and choices.

How is your heart? What, or who, has your heart right now? How does that show itself in your life?

Respond:
Draw a picture of your heart. What does it look like right now? What is its shape? What is its color? What is within it? Where is God in the midst of it? How is he shaping and forming and molding your heart?

Rest:
Give your heart completely to Jesus. Allow him to hold it in His strong and loving hands. Rest there in his love, care, and strength.

Thirty-Three

Read:
Jesus left that place and went to the vicinity of Tyre. He entered a house and did not want anyone to know it; yet he could not keep his presence secret. In fact, as soon as she heard about him, a woman whose little daughter was possessed by an evil spirit came and fell at his feet. The

woman was a Greek, born in Syrian Phoenicia. She begged Jesus to drive the demon out of her daughter.

"First let the children eat all they want," he told her, "for it is not right to take the children's bread and toss it to their dogs."

"Yes, Lord," she replied, "but even the dogs under the table eat the children's crumbs."

Then he told her, "For such a reply, you may go; the demon has left your daughter."

She went home and found her child lying on the bed, and the demon gone. (Mark 7:24-30)

Reflect:

Attitude is everything…or so they say. It's a familiar phrase and, in the case of the gospel, one that would appear to be as accurate as it is familiar. So much of this life seems to be determined by our attitude. And so much of what Jesus was willing to do (or not do) for the person standing in front of him at the time, had to do with the attitude of their heart.

The Pharisees, for example, had an attitude. They had an extremely high opinion of themselves; being really concerned about position and prestige, status and importance. They were a proud bunch to be sure. And because of their knowledge of the Scriptures, their perceived wisdom, and their personal piety, they felt like they deserved something special from God. In other words, they were entitled.

Entitlement is an ugly thing. It is an attitude of self-importance, and pride, and arrogance. It makes us believe that we really deserve some kind of special treatment, special privilege, or special consideration. Therefore it leads to all kinds of problems in our hearts. To be entitled is *"to have a right or claim to something."* Therefore, if you have a spirit of entitlement, life (or people, or God) owes you something.

This feeling of entitlement breeds a sense of demandingness within us. When someone is entitled, they demand to be treated in a certain way. And Jesus didn't typically respond too well to people with a spirit of entitlement or demandingness. Those that were fueled by such an attitude didn't seem to get very far with him. But those with a spirit of brokenness and humility were the ones that Jesus went out of his way to help.

Enter the woman from Syrian Phoenicia. Her *little daughter was possessed by an evil spirit.* This woman had just such a spirit. In fact, she was a Greek, not a part of "God's chosen people"—Israel—at all. She was an outsider, an alien, a nobody…and she knew it. She was not entitled, not deserving, not demanding. She was just a desperate mother pleading for the healing of her little girl. And her approach to Jesus is saturated with that attitude—*she came and fell at his feet.* It is so beautiful! People with a spirit of demandingness and entitlement do not fall at anyone's feet, they march right in. But here she is, face to the ground, in front of the Savior— begging.

Jesus, fully realizing the state of her heart, makes a statement that on the surface seems harsh, but, when rightly understood, is actually the direct opposite of that. It is a statement that is filled with gentleness, playfulness and care. His intent is to allow the purity and truth of her heart to shine through. By using the image of the family pet sitting under the table waiting for the children's crumbs, he hopes to make it clear to everyone that she fully realizes her position, which endears her to his heart. It is such a contrast from the demanding, entitled Pharisees. And such a statement: that God is the God of all, not just the nation of Israel.

Her response is not defensive or defiant, or even resistant. She acknowledges that what Jesus has just said is indeed true. She does not deserve his favor. She does not deserve a single thing. She is just begging for his grace and mercy. And wouldn't you know it, because she was begging, and not demanding, she receives exactly what she was seeking: healing, wholeness, and peace. Thanks be to God!

Respond:
Search your heart in prayer and ask God to reveal any entitlement or demandingness that may be within you. What do you see? How are you like the Pharisees? Where are you demanding of God? And how are you like the woman from Syrian Phoenicia? Where are you on your knees begging? Ask God to continue to transform your heart into one like this woman.

Rest:
For the next few minutes try to let go of all entitlement and demandingness as best you are able. And rest in the arms of His love and mercy.

Thirty-Four

Read:
Then Jesus left the vicinity of Tyre and went through Sidon, down to the Sea of Galilee and into the region of the Decapolis. There some people brought to him a man who was deaf and could hardly talk, and they begged him to place his hand on the man.

After he took him aside, away from the crowd, Jesus put his fingers into the man's ears. Then he spit and touched the man's tongue. He looked up to heaven and with a deep sigh said to him, "Ephphatha!" (which means, "Be opened!"). At this, the man's ears were opened, his tongue was loosened and he began to speak plainly.

Jesus commanded them not to tell anyone. But the more he did so, the more they kept talking about it. People were overwhelmed with amazement. "He has done everything well," they said. "He even makes the deaf hear and the mute speak." (Mark 7:31-37)

Reflect:

It is amazing how, if you are paying careful attention, one little word can communicate so much. In this case it is the word *sigh*. Jesus had just come into contact with a man who was deaf and could hardly speak. We are not told if he had been this way since birth or if, at some point in time, disease or disaster had reared its ugly head and taken away that which most of us take for granted.

Just try and imagine for a moment what his life must've been like? Not knowing the joy of hearing a beautifully played song, or the sound of the birds in the trees, or the rain on the roof. Not being able to enjoy the sound of the surf on the beach, or of a mountain stream, or the laughter of a child. Not being able to have a leisurely conversation, or clearly say the words *I love you* to those who matter most. Can you imagine having the feeling every second of every day that you were missing out?

And on top of all that, can you imagine enduring all the stares and pointing, and maybe even outright laughter, whenever you did finally try to communicate with someone. Because no matter how hard you tried the words just wouldn't seem to come out. This was the life of the man that *some people* brought to Jesus that day. And they begged Jesus to place his hand upon their friend, to restore his hearing and speech, and to make him whole once again.

Jesus certainly didn't disappoint. He took the man aside, away from the crowd. This poor soul had certainly had his fill of being the center of attention—the freak. Jesus wanted to make sure that that didn't happen again. After taking him aside, he looked deeply into the man's eyes (one of the ways he could still communicate) and *put his fingers into the man's ears, then he spit and touched the man's tongue.* How beautiful. Jesus was *placing his hand* on the very parts of this man's life that had caused him so much pain and anguish.

And then it happened. Jesus looked up to heaven and gave a *deep sigh*. You might be saying, "So what? What is so significant about that?" It is significant because of the emotion the word captures. It is significant because it is Mark's way of describing what is actually going on in the heart of God. It is significant because the words *deep sigh* are actually better translated as *deep groan*. It was something that came up from the very core of Jesus' being.

It was a sound that—although not a word—communicated so much; both to the deaf man, as well as all those looking on. This groan was a mixture of both sadness and frustration. This groan said to everyone: "it didn't have to be this way. This wasn't the way it was intended to be." It was a groan that shows us all that our brokenness breaks the heart of our God. He cares deeply about our pain and he wants nothing more than to reach out his hand and touch our broken places; making them whole once again.

Respond:
What are your broken places? What areas of your life cause you great pain? How do you think God feels about those? Do you think he cares? How does it make you feel to know that God groans over your pain? And that God longs to place his hand on those parts of your life in such a way that it can make all things whole again.

Rest:
In prayer, allow God to tenderly place his hand on the broken places of your heart and soul. Rest there in his healing touch.

Thirty-Five

Read:
During those days another large crowd gathered. Since they had nothing to eat, Jesus called his disciples to him and said, "I have compassion for these people; they have already been with me three days and have nothing to eat. If I send them home hungry, they will collapse on the way, because some of them have come a long distance."

His disciples answered, "But where in this remote place can anyone get enough bread to feed them?"

"How many loaves do you have?" Jesus asked.

"Seven," they replied.

He told the crowd to sit down on the ground. When he had taken the seven loaves and given thanks, he broke them and gave them to his disciples to set before the people, and they did so. They had a few small fish as well; he gave thanks for them also and told the disciples to distribute them. The people ate and were satisfied. Afterward the disciples picked up seven basketfuls of broken pieces that were left over. About four thousand men were present. And having sent them away, he got into the boat with his disciples and went to the region of Dalmanutha. (Mark 8:1-10)

Reflect:
Do you think they had even a vague sense of *deja vu* as they passed through the crowd with the bits of loaves and fish? I mean it hadn't been all that long ago that this very same thing happened once before. After all, feeding thousands of people with a couple of loaves and a few fish doesn't happen every day, right? It really makes you wonder what the disciples must've been thinking.

And even more it makes you wonder what Jesus was up to. Why the repetition? Was he simply responding to what the situation called for, or was there something specific Jesus was trying to teach his disciples? He was so intentional about all he did. Each act was not just a miracle, but a teachable moment as well. Was he trying to get some point across that required repetition in order to be fully made? A very wise man once said, "Every parable of Jesus was a miracle of wisdom, and every miracle a parable of teaching" (Dr. Arthur T. Pierson). So we can be sure that Jesus had, not only the hungry crowd in mind, but his disciples as well...and you...and me.

I know that at times it can take something happening more than once before its significance really begins to sink in. And what a foreshadowing of the future this act was—a glimpse of what they would be doing after Jesus left this world and returned to the Father. They would be the ones feeding the hungry multitudes with the bread of life.

I wonder as they traveled from town to town in Acts if the image of feeding the hungry crowds with Jesus ever returned to their minds, and brought them comfort or encouragement? We can't really be sure what Jesus was really up to that day, but you can bet he was up to something. Just like today...in each of our lives. He is at work, whether we understand it fully or not. Rest assured, He is at work.

Respond:
Take some time right now to reflect on your life, your circumstances, and your relationships. How is God at work? What is he up to, both in you and through you? What are your places of struggle and/or challenge? How might God be using those things to mold and form you? Write it all down in your journal.

Rest:
Take a few minutes and rest in the knowledge that He is, indeed, at work in your life and in your world. And he will accomplish his purposes both in you and through you.

Thirty-Six

Read:
The Pharisees came and began to question Jesus. To test him, they asked him for a sign from heaven. He sighed deeply and said, "Why does this generation ask for a miraculous sign? I tell you the truth, no sign will be given to it." Then he left them, got back into the boat and crossed to the other side. (Mark 8:11-13)

Reflect:
The Pharisees were questioning Jesus—asking for a sign from heaven. Their questioning, however, wasn't particularly sincere. In fact, it clearly states that they were testing him; trying to determine whether or not he gained their seal of approval. Because, ultimately, they wanted to be the

ones in control; they were looking for a God who would behave as they wanted. Can you imagine the arrogance?

Jesus, however, would not play their games. He was not interested in being controlled. He was glad to give all kinds of signs to the sincere seeker, but not willing to give any to those who were demanding or manipulative. As a matter of fact, to them he said, *"No sign will be given."* Can you blame him? What would you have done? And what, exactly, is the lesson here that he's trying to get across?

Is it that Jesus will always come to us on our turf, but only on his terms? Is it that He is the one in control and will not give it up? Or is it that we can't just demand that God behave the way we want and expect him to actually show up?

The point seems to be that when we try and dictate how and when God *must* come to us and what he *must* do for us, we stop seeking him altogether. At that point we are only seeking our own agenda. And when we are only seeking our own agenda, we are no longer seeking God at all.

Respond:
Where do you struggle most with control issues in your life? What does that look like? What form does it take? Where do you struggle most with God's control? What would it mean to fully trust his control in those areas of your life?

Rest:
Rest in God's loving control of your life. As sit before him in silence and pray, slowly open your hands, symbolizing your willingness to let go of the need to control those areas.

Thirty-Seven

Read:
The disciples had forgotten to bring bread, except for one loaf they had with them in the boat. "Be careful," Jesus warned them. "Watch out for the yeast of the Pharisees and that of Herod."

They discussed this with one another and said, "It is because we have no bread."

Aware of their discussion, Jesus asked them: "Why are you talking about having no bread? Do you still not see or understand? Are your hearts hardened? Do you have eyes but fail to see, and ears but fail to hear? And don't you remember? When I broke the five loaves for the five thousand, how many basketfuls of pieces did you pick up?"

"Twelve," they replied.

"And when I broke the seven loaves for the four thousand, how many basketfuls of pieces did you pick up?"

They answered, "Seven."
He said to them, "Do you still not understand?" (Mark 8:14-21)

Reflect:
The disciples had forgotten. What a statement. A man much wiser than I once said that the three greatest enemies of the spiritual life are: inertia, amnesia, and manãna. I couldn't agree more. In fact, each of these three enemies has reared its ugly head more often than I care to admit over the past 30+ years of my spiritual journey.

Lack of movement, lack of memory, and lack of initiative have all been the cause of significant struggle in my spiritual life at one time or another. And it appears that I'm in good company. All through the scriptures men and women of faith have fought the very same battles. In fact, here in this section of Mark's gospel we vividly see that even the disciples had their struggles, particularly with enemy number two: amnesia.

They had just left the region of the Decapolis where Jesus had, for the second time, fed and enormous amount of people with a few barley loaves and some small fish. Yet as soon as they got into the boat they began to worry about having no bread. Can you believe that? What must have been going through Jesus' mind at that moment? If it were me, I'd have been thinking: *Are you kidding me? Have you all been completely asleep the past few days? Could your memory possibly be that short?*

But Jesus is much more patient and kind than I am. Instead of becoming frustrated, he makes his point with clarity, precision, and wisdom as he proceeds to remind them of the events of the past few days. He does this in a unique and engaging way—by asking them questions. In fact he asks them seven consecutive questions—all of which are incredibly insightful. But one in particular that might be the most telling of all: *Don't you remember?*

Don't you remember when I fed the five thousand? And don't you remember (moments ago) when I fed the four thousand? You were there for both of these. You even passed out the food. Do you still not understand? I love you. I am faithful to provide for you. Trust me.

So much of the life of faith has to do with simply remembering. Remembering all of the times, and all of the ways, and all of the places in which God has been faithful to care for us and to provide for our needs. And as we continue to remind ourselves of God's goodness and God's faithfulness, trust begins to spring up and take root within our hearts.

Respond:
Look back on your life and draw a timeline, remembering the times and the situations and the circumstances where God has really shown up in a significant way. What are the times and places in your life where God has shown himself to be faithful to you?

Rest:
Take a few minutes and simply rest in Him: rest in his care, rest in his faithfulness, rest in his unfailing love.

Thirty-Eight

Read:
They came to Bethsaida, and some people brought a blind man and begged Jesus to touch him. He took the blind man by the hand and led him outside the village. When he had spit on the man's eyes and put his hands on him, Jesus asked, "Do you see anything?"

He looked up and said, "I see people; they look like trees walking around."

Once more Jesus put his hands on the man's eyes. Then his eyes were opened, his sight was restored, and he saw everything clearly. Jesus sent him home, saying, "Don't go into the village." (Mark 8:22-26)

Reflect:
The entire eighth chapter of Mark is about *seeing*. Not just seeing in the physical sense, but seeing in a much larger sense—perceiving, understanding, "getting it." That is the context for this particular miracle. Jesus is not just healing a blind man; he is teaching his disciples the truth about their own spiritual vision. As we have said before, Jesus is operating on so many different levels at the same time—he is so intentional about all he does, even in the miracles he performs.

In this particular case, the man that is blind is healed in *stages*. The first touch allows him to be able to see, but not too clearly—he sees people but *they look like trees walking around*. And then the second touch totally restores his sight and he is able to see *everything clearly*. Thus, the intent of the two touches is to show his disciples that their sight too is being restored—in stages. It is to show them that slowly, with each day and each new experience with Jesus, they too are *seeing* a little more clearly. That piece-by-piece and bit-by-bit they are actually beginning to "get it." And it could be that we are too.

Respond:
How has your spiritual *seeing* changed in the past year? What is clearer to you now than it has been before? What have been the places, and the ways, and the experiences of the past year that Jesus has used to touch your eyes and make you see more clearly?

Rest:
For the next few minutes imagine Jesus kneeling down in front of you and placing his hands gently on your eyes. Rest in his healing touch, with the knowledge that he, indeed, is touching your eyes and restoring your vision.

Thirty-Nine

Read:
Jesus and his disciples went on to the villages around Caesarea Philippi. On the way he asked them, "Who do people say I am?"
They replied, "Some say John the Baptist; others say Elijah; and still others, one of the prophets."
"But what about you?" he asked. "Who do you say I am?"
Peter answered, "You are the Christ."
Jesus warned them not to tell anyone about him. (Mark 8:27-30)

Reflect:
The questions Jesus asks in scripture are simply masterful. They are questions that aren't just relevant to those to whom they were first asked, but just as relevant to us today. They are questions that always seem to require something of us: at times reflection, and at times vulnerability, but always a response. They are questions that cut right to the heart of the matter; and this case is certainly no exception.

As Jesus and his friends walk along the road, he turns to them—the ones that know him best—and asks two remarkably simple, yet incredibly profound questions. The first being, *"Who do people say that I am?"* addressing once again the whole notion seeing—perceiving and understanding.

In response, his friends tell Jesus who those around them say that He is. Then Jesus turns directly toward them—his very best friends—and asks them, point blank, their thoughts own on the subject. *"But what about you? Who do you say I am?"*

Jesus is not asking them for the right theological answer. No, it is way more personal than that. He is asking them who he is *to them.* And every time we read these words, we need to realize that he is asking us the same thing.

Respond:
Put yourself in the shoes of the disciples. You and Jesus are walking down a quiet road on a beautiful fall day. As you walk along, in a peaceful silence, he turns to you and asks…*"What about you? Who do you say I am?"* What is your response? Tell Jesus about it. Write it down in your journal.

Rest:
Take your answer to the question above and rest in it. Rest in the fact that
Jesus is that to you. Just be with him in that truth.

Forty

Read:
*He then began to teach them that the Son of Man must suffer many
things and be rejected by the elders, chief priests and teachers of the law,
and that he must be killed and after three days rise again. He spoke
plainly about this, and Peter took him aside and began to rebuke him.*

*But when Jesus turned and looked at his disciples, he rebuked Peter.
"Get behind me, Satan!" he said. "You do not have in mind the things of
God, but the things of men."*

*Then he called the crowd to him along with his disciples and said: "If
anyone would come after me, he must deny himself and take up his cross
and follow me. For whoever wants to save his life will lose it, but whoever
loses his life for me and for the gospel will save it. What good is it for a
man to gain the whole world, yet forfeit his soul? Or what can a man give
in exchange for his soul? If anyone is ashamed of me and my words in
this adulterous and sinful generation, the Son of Man will be ashamed of
him when he comes in his Father's glory with the holy angels." (Mark 8:31-
38)*

Reflect:
The true nature of the gospel is radical, extremely counter-cultural. So
much so that it is easy, if we are not careful, to get seduced into believing a
version of the gospel that is much safer, much more vanilla than the one
proclaimed by Jesus. It is easy to talk ourselves (and others) into believing
that we can truly follow Jesus and still pretty much be like everyone else
around us.

Jesus knew this well. He knew how incredibly high the demands of the
gospel were—calling for total surrender, total abandonment of our own
wills and ways. And he also knew how easily we would be led astray by
more attractive distortions of the truth—ones that make it possible for us to
have and to hold all of the things the world sees as valuable while, at the
same time, claiming to be his followers.

We have to look no further than these verses to find a prime example of
this in Simon Peter. In this instance he is exhibit A of this type of thinking.
In fact, Peter is so convinced of his misguided ways that he actually has
the gall to take Jesus aside and rebuke him for talking about being called
to death and sacrifice and suffering and pain. I wonder if he was mostly
trying to convince himself that there was an easier way. Jesus, however,
was never about the easier way, he was always about the better way;

giving Peter a firm rebuke for his efforts with the scathing words, "*Get behind me, Satan! You do not have in mind the things of God, but the things of men.*"

Then Jesus proceeds to tell the whole crowd what *having in mind the things of God* looks like—and that it, indeed, looks very different from *having in mind the things of men*. As a matter of fact, it is the exact opposite. Having in mind the *things of God* includes denying yourself, taking up your cross, and following Jesus. In other words it involves being selfless, sacrificial, and submissive—three things that the world around us is not real high on.

Having in mind the *things of God* involves losing your life for the sake of Jesus; for the sake of his kingdom. It involves a life that does not revolve around making a name for ourselves, or winning popularity contests, or acquiring positions and prestige and power. It does not involve accumulating a lot of stuff for our own personal enjoyment. What it does involve is a life saturated with God—rather than a life stuffed with self.

So the real question is, "Are we up for it? Are we in?"

Respond:
As you listen to these words of Jesus what does it do within you? How does it make you feel? Does it touch either a fear or a longing deep within you? What is your response? Write it down in your journal. What does it look like for you personally to live your life by these verses? In prayer, ask God to show you what he wants both for you and from you.

Rest:
Spend a few minutes sitting before God with open hands, in total surrender. Rest in both his care for you and his desire for you.

Forty-One

Read:
And he said to them, "*I tell you the truth, some who are standing here will not taste death before they see the kingdom of God come with power.*"

After six days Jesus took Peter, James and John with him and led them up a high mountain, where they were all alone. There he was transfigured before them. His clothes became dazzling white, whiter than anyone in the world could bleach them. And there appeared before them Elijah and Moses, who were talking with Jesus.

Peter said to Jesus, "Rabbi, it is good for us to be here. Let us put up three shelters—one for you, one for Moses and one for Elijah." (He did not know what to say, they were so frightened.)

Then a cloud appeared and enveloped them, and a voice came from the cloud: "This is my Son, whom I love. Listen to him!"

Suddenly, when they looked around, they no longer saw anyone with them except Jesus.

As they were coming down the mountain, Jesus gave them orders not to tell anyone what they had seen until the Son of Man had risen from the dead. They kept the matter to themselves, discussing what "rising from the dead" meant.

And they asked him, "Why do the teachers of the law say that Elijah must come first?"

Jesus replied, "To be sure, Elijah does come first, and restores all things. Why then is it written that the Son of Man must suffer much and be rejected? But I tell you, Elijah has come, and they have done to him everything they wished, just as it is written about him." (Mark 9:1-13)

Reflect:
Sometimes it's difficult to see clearly in the midst of our own life's circumstances. During such times the struggle and turmoil of day-to-day existence allows us only to be able to see what is right in front of us—which can leave us both overwhelmed and paralyzed. What we need is someone that can take us up above the clouds and the chaos of this life, to higher ground where we can see everything in proper perspective. What we need is someone to take us to a place where our vision, as well as our lives, can be transformed.

That is the gift Jesus gives his three closest friends on this day. He gives them the gift of the mountaintop. The mountaintop is the place high above the noise and hustle and bustle of the crowd. The mountaintop is the place where we can see things as they really are—or better yet, as they were intended to be.

On the mountaintop Jesus shows the disciples himself in a way they had never seen him before. He shows them himself as he really is. It is on top of this mountain that he draws back the curtain of his humanity and gives his friends a small glimpse of his divinity—his glory.

And if that weren't enough, standing on either side of Him are two of Israel's biggest heroes: Moses (the giver of the Law) and Elijah (one of the greatest prophets). Both of whom spoke intimately with God during their time on earth. These were the legends of the faith. They were men the disciples had only heard about in stories and read about in the Scriptures, but now, here they were, standing right in front of them.

And to top it all off, there was the cloud (just like the Israelites had experienced during their journey through the desert) and the Voice (identifying Jesus, once again, as God's beloved Son and exhorting the disciples to listen to him).

When the three friends of Jesus see all of this they are both thrilled and terrified at the same time. What's going on in the valley below is now the furthest thing from their minds. After all, they are with Jesus, and everything else had completely faded from their minds. There was nothing they wanted more than to stay right where they were and soak it all in.

It can be the same for each of us. Each day Jesus invites us to journey up to the mountaintop. To follow him to the place where our vision can become clear and we can see him as he really is. To simply be with him in a place where it's just the two of us, no interruptions, no distractions. To be with him in a place where we can seek his face and listen for his voice, a place where we can spend intimate time with him each day in a way that completely captures our hearts and changes everything about us.

You and I are invited, this very day. Please don't miss the chance to follow him to that place where the skies are clear and the air is fresh. It is truly a place of transformation.

Respond:
What do you think it would have been like to be on that mountain? What would you have been thinking? What would you have been feeling? How do you think you would have responded? How do you respond now?

Rest:
Simply rest in the presence of Jesus as you enjoy the peace and beauty of the mountaintop.

Forty-Two

Read:
When they came to the other disciples, they saw a large crowd around them and the teachers of the law arguing with them. As soon as all the people saw Jesus, they were overwhelmed with wonder and ran to greet him.

"What are you arguing with them about?" he asked.

A man in the crowd answered, "Teacher, I brought you my son, who is possessed by a spirit that has robbed him of speech. Whenever it seizes him, it throws him to the ground. He foams at the mouth, gnashes his teeth and becomes rigid. I asked your disciples to drive out the spirit, but they could not."

"O unbelieving generation," Jesus replied, "how long shall I stay with you? How long shall I put up with you? Bring the boy to me."

So they brought him. When the spirit saw Jesus, it immediately threw the boy into a convulsion. He fell to the ground and rolled around, foaming at the mouth.

Jesus asked the boy's father, "How long has he been like this?"

"From childhood," he answered. "It has often thrown him into fire or water to kill him. But if you can do anything, take pity on us and help us."

" 'If you can'?" said Jesus. "Everything is possible for him who believes."

Immediately the boy's father exclaimed, "I do believe; help me overcome my unbelief!"

When Jesus saw that a crowd was running to the scene, he rebuked the evil spirit. "You deaf and mute spirit," he said, "I command you, come out of him and never enter him again."

The spirit shrieked, convulsed him violently and came out. The boy looked so much like a corpse that many said, "He's dead." But Jesus took him by the hand and lifted him to his feet, and he stood up.

After Jesus had gone indoors, his disciples asked him privately, "Why couldn't we drive it out?"

He replied, "This kind can come out only by prayer."
(Mark 9:14-29)

Reflect:

It is the cry of each of our hearts at one time or another, if we are completely honest. It is a cry that voices the all too familiar tension between faith and doubt...*I believe; help me overcome my unbelief!"* And at its core it is really a prayer—a desperate plea to God—begging him to take the tiny bit of belief that dwells within our hearts and grow it into something bigger and more substantial; something big enough and substantial enough to be trusted, to be relied upon.

But logic would say, "How can both exist at the same time? Are they not mutually exclusive? Can there really be belief and unbelief in one heart simultaneously?"

But our hearts know the truth, because our hearts are not bound by logic—they go far beyond. As Augustine once said so beautifully, "The heart has reasons which reason knows not of." And anyone who knows the heart of a loving and desperate father understands exactly what Augustine (as well as the man in Mark 9) meant. It is a heart that says, "I believe. I really do. But this is my very own son; the one who means more to me than anything on earth. Therefore, please help me to not only believe, but to really trust you—even with the most important thing in my life!"

Respond:

Where are you struggling with the tension between faith and doubt? Is there room in you for both? Where in your life are you praying the prayer, *I believe; help me overcome my unbelief?*

Rest:

For the next few minutes bring your tensions of belief and doubt to God and place them in his strong, and loving, and utterly trustworthy hands.

Forty-Three

Read:
They left that place and passed through Galilee. Jesus did not want anyone to know where they were, because he was teaching his disciples. He said to them, "The Son of Man is going to be betrayed into the hands of men. They will kill him, and after three days he will rise." But they did not understand what he meant and were afraid to ask him about it. (Mark 9:30-32)

Reflect:
When you've got something really important to share with those you love, what do you do? How do you go about it? Most likely you get away—go to a place where you are with them and them alone, a place where you will not be interrupted. You go to great lengths to eliminate all the distractions and create a space that gives you the best possibility that the words you have to share are going to be heard; and once they have been heard, that they are going to be considered and received.

That is what Jesus is trying to accomplish in this instance. He *did not want anyone to know where they were* simply because his message was of the utmost urgency. It was imperative for them to be attentive and focused so they could clearly hear his words and then begin to wrestle with both their meaning and their implications; for his time with them was quickly drawing to a close.

His betrayal and death were drawing near and when the time for both was at hand he didn't want it to surprise or confuse them. He didn't want the unfolding of his final days and hours to throw them into doubt and despair, for they were the ones who would eventually carry his message forward into all the world: his message of mercy and grace and hope, his message of forgiveness and restoration and life, his message of God's incredible love for a people that are constantly turning away from him.

This was the entire reason Jesus had come into this world—to give his life in love for his beloved children. It would be a message that, over the next several days, they would hear over and over again in hopes that when the day of his passion finally arrived, they might truly understand and might be truly prepared for the days ahead. Because eventually they would be called on to give up their lives as well.

Respond:
Put yourself in the disciple's shoes. Imagine you have been following Jesus for a couple of years and have come to know him well, to love him deeply, and to depend on him fully. One day he turns to you and tells you he is getting ready to be betrayed and killed. How does it make you feel? What do you want to say to him? What do you want to do? Do you get a

sense that he may be calling you to have the same attitude? Where or how is he asking you to give yourself for the kingdom?

Rest:
Spend some time in gratitude, thanking Jesus for what he has done for you. Rest in his grace and forgiveness.

Forty-Four

Read:
They came to Capernaum. When he was in the house, he asked them, "What were you arguing about on the road?" But they kept quiet because on the way they had argued about who was the greatest.

Sitting down, Jesus called the Twelve and said, "If anyone wants to be first, he must be the very last, and the servant of all."

He took a little child and had him stand among them. Taking him in his arms, he said to them, "Whoever welcomes one of these little children in my name welcomes me; and whoever welcomes me does not welcome me but the one who sent me." (Mark 9:33-37)

Reflect:
If I'm completely honest I have to admit it. I have to confess that I too, in the parts of my heart that I don't want anyone to know about, have a deep desire to be the greatest. I would probably never use that exact word and I would probably never want to be that obvious in my pursuit of it (and would be just as embarrassed as the disciples were if someone found me out) but I have to admit that deep inside I have an overwhelming desire to be significant. As sad as it is to have to say, I long to be recognized, and to be admired, and to be seen as the best. As a matter of fact I work pretty hard at trying to attain those very things, using the very gifts God has given me to, in some warped way, attempt to prove to myself and others that I am valuable, that I am worthwhile, that I am enough.

I suppose that each of us has our own reasons for such a thing. For me I wonder if the reason I try so hard to prove my worth is because I'm terrified deep down that I really don't have any. I'm terrified that I might be of no value—insignificant, unimportant, not enough.

So I guess I can't really criticize the disciples for their behavior, because in my heart I know that I am right there with them. I may not be as blatantly obvious in my efforts as they, but nonetheless I desperately and continuously seek significance and security in very subtle, and some not so subtle, ways.

It is in the midst of this very struggle that Jesus enters the picture—he comes along and shows us a new way. He shows us that he is the only one that can give us true value. In love, he bestows upon us our worth and our identity. He lets us know that we are his Beloved. He lets us know that we are of infinite value and worth in his eyes because we are his and he loves what he has made. He loves us with a love that knows no limits. This is the truth he wants us to live our lives from.

And when we live our lives guided by this truth we are finally able to understand what he means when he says that the last will be first. Since our value and worth are rooted in him and his immense love, we are free to love others with the same love in which we ourselves are loved. We no longer have to work so hard at making ourselves worthy; we no longer have to be consumed with ourselves. We can actually make ourselves last in order to truly love others by making them first. We are free to elevate them above ourselves, instead of having to compare and compete. Others are no longer a threat to our own personal value—we are now able to love freely like a child, because we are loved as his child.

Respond:
How do you try to get your needs for significance met? How do you try to make yourself feel valuable? Fill in the blank: I feel most significant when_____. What does it mean to find your identity in Jesus?

Rest:
Spend a few minutes simply resting in God's great love for you.

Forty-Five

Read:
"Teacher," said John, "we saw a man driving out demons in your name and we told him to stop, because he was not one of us."

"Do not stop him," Jesus said. "No one who does a miracle in my name can in the next moment say anything bad about me, for whoever is not against us is for us. I tell you the truth, anyone who gives you a cup of water in my name because you belong to Christ will certainly not lose his reward.

"And if anyone causes one of these little ones who believe in me to sin, it would be better for him to be thrown into the sea with a large millstone tied around his neck. If your hand causes you to sin, cut it off. It is better for you to enter life maimed than with two hands to go into hell, where the fire never goes out. And if your foot causes you to sin, cut it off. It is better for you to enter life crippled than to have two feet and be thrown into hell. And if your eye causes you to sin, pluck it out. It is better for you to enter the kingdom of God with one eye than to have two eyes and be thrown into hell, where

'their worm does not die, and the fire is not quenched.'

Everyone will be salted with fire.
   "Salt is good, but if it loses its saltiness, how can you make it salty again? Have salt in yourselves, and be at peace with each other." (Mark 9:38-50)

Reflect:

You don't have to look very far into the pages of Scripture before you see how much God hates sin. In fact, whenever he addresses the subject his words are always strong and intense—even harsh. He wants it to be perfectly clear to us exactly what the negative effects of sin are. He wants us to completely understand that sin always brings about death. In fact, *the wages of sin is death* (Romans 6:23).

Therefore he urges us to avoid sin at all costs, no matter what lengths we have to go to—even if it requires a *cutting off* or a *plucking out*. Better to *cut off* or *pluck out* than to be totally and completely separated from God for all eternity. For God hates sin and will not tolerate its presence. This means that in order for us to be able to come into his presence we must be completely free of it—totally cleansed.

That is where the beauty of the cross comes shining through. God takes our sin (as well as the penalty for it) upon himself. That is the incredible message of the gospel—in Jesus we are perfectly clean, absolutely forgiven. It is a message of life and hope, of redemption and reconciliation, of mercy and grace, of deep forgiveness and unconditional love. Who could ask for anything more?

Respond:

How do these words of Jesus make you feel? What do they do within you? Is there anything in your life that needs to be *cut off* or *plucked out*?

Confess your sins to God right now. Not just your behavior, but also the attitudes beneath the behavior. Write it all down on a piece of paper. Give it all to God and ask his forgiveness. Now tear the piece of paper up in little pieces and throw it away. God has taken away your sin, and he remembers it no more (Hebrews 8:12).

Rest:

Rest in his forgiveness.

Forty-Six

Read:

Jesus then left that place and went into the region of Judea and across the Jordan. Again crowds of people came to him, and as was his custom, he taught them.

Some Pharisees came and tested him by asking, "Is it lawful for a man to divorce his wife?"

"What did Moses command you?" he replied.

They said, "Moses permitted a man to write a certificate of divorce and send her away."

"It was because your hearts were hard that Moses wrote you this law," Jesus replied. "But at the beginning of creation God 'made them male and female. 'For this reason a man will leave his father and mother and be united to his wife, and the two will become one flesh.' So they are no longer two, but one. Therefore what God has joined together, let man not separate."

When they were in the house again, the disciples asked Jesus about this. He answered, "Anyone who divorces his wife and marries another woman commits adultery against her. And if she divorces her husband and marries another man, she commits adultery." (Mark 10:1-12)

Reflect:

I have wonderfully vivid memories of my wedding day. Even though it was some thirty years ago, I can still clearly see my beautiful bride as the doors in the back of the church opened and she stood there, radiant— seeing her in a way I had never seen her before, beautifully dressed in an amazing white dress that was draped just off her tanned shoulders. She simply took my breath away. And if the truth be known, she still does.

Because as wonderful as that day was—to have all of the people you love the most in one place to celebrate your union with the woman you long to spend the rest of your life with—our wedding day was only the beginning. It was an incredible beginning, to say the least, but still only the beginning. Because the very best part of having a wedding day is the marriage that follows. In fact, the whole reason you have a wedding day is because of what comes after it.

The point is that as much as I loved that wedding day, I have loved the life my wife and I have gotten to share even more. In fact, the very best moments of my life have all involved my relationship with her and our love for each other. Be it a romantic walk at sunset on the Battery in Charleston or a beautiful day on a deserted beach on the island of St. John, there have just been so many experiences and memories and moments that we have been fortunate enough to share together that have formed our hearts and made us who we are. And there have been plenty of ordinary days and lots of everyday life as well.

For thirty wonderful years we have had the privilege of doing life together, during which time we have had four incredible children. It has been a life so rich and full that at times I have thought to myself, "I'm so full that if I were a balloon I would burst."

I think that this is the reason marriage seems to hold such a special place in the heart of God. Because ultimately what God longs for with each of us is not just a wedding day, but a marriage. He wants, not only a moment when we look at him and say "I do," but also a life in which we continuously choose to make a commitment to be completely his.

It's almost as if marriage offers a window through which we are able to see God's heart—his deep love and affection for us, his beloved bride. Through the window of marriage we see a hint of both his hope for, and his desire for, inconceivable depths of intimacy in our relationship with Him—an intimacy that we long for at the very core of our being, and yet an intimacy that we could not even imagine possible in our wildest dreams.

Ultimately that is what marriage is all about—union. It is about the union between a man and wife, which gives us the most concrete and tangible picture possible of the life God really desires with each of us. You can almost hear the love and tenderness in the voice of Jesus as he talks about it: *"For this reason a man will leave his father and mother and be united to his wife, and the two will become one flesh. So they are no longer two, but one."*

That is his greatest hope for us—that we might become one with him; God and his people in intimate union. It is such a beautiful dream; so beautiful in fact that it actually inspires the very first words of poetry—*flesh of my flesh and bone of my bone*. It's almost as if only the words of poetry could possibly begin to capture the mystery of it all.

Respond:
Why do you think God has a special place in his heart for marriage? Would you say that a *wedding day* or a *marriage* best describes your experience with God thus far? What would it look like for your relationship with God to be more like a marriage? What kind of vows would you write for that marriage?

Rest:
Spend a few minutes just being with your beloved God.

Forty-Seven

Read:
People were bringing little children to Jesus to have him touch them, but the disciples rebuked them. When Jesus saw this, he was indignant. He said to them, "Let the little children come to me, and do not hinder them,

for the kingdom of God belongs to such as these. I tell you the truth, anyone who will not receive the kingdom of God like a little child will never enter it." And he took the children in his arms, put his hands on them and blessed them. (Mark 10:13-16)

Reflect:
What do you suppose it would look like to *receive the kingdom of God like a little child*? Would it involve a certain capacity to trust? Or do you think it might have something to do with the ability to give and receive affection freely; in a way that only a child seems able to do?

Do you suppose it has something to do with the capability to live completely in the moment, with no worries or distractions—to take things as they come? Or is it something about having an attitude of playfulness and joy? Something involving the ease with which we laugh or cry?

Or could it be something to do with the art, and the beauty, and the innocence of being totally yourself—before this world has gotten a hold of you and tried to teach you that being yourself is just not good enough? Or maybe it is all of the above.

Whatever it is, Jesus absolutely adored children. He loved them so much that they caused his arms to fly open and his hands to reach out. They just seemed to bring him to life—to bring a smile to his lips and joy to his heart. Something in their attitude and in their innocence was exactly what he was looking for, just what he was hoping the rest of us would see and discover and live by. That *something* is what we must consider. It is what we must recapture and what we must try to understand…if we have any hope of entering the kingdom, that is.

Respond:
What do you think are the qualities of a child that Jesus most loved and appreciated? Which of these qualities do you see in yourself? In others around you? In what ways is God asking you to become more childlike today? How will you do this?

Rest:
Simply be in the moment with God right now. Receive whatever it is he has for you. Rest in it.

Forty-Eight

Read:
As Jesus started on his way, a man ran up to him and fell on his knees before him. "Good teacher," he asked, "what must I do to inherit eternal life?"

"Why do you call me good?" Jesus answered. "No one is good—except God alone. You know the commandments: 'Do not murder, do not commit adultery, do not steal, do not give false testimony, do not defraud, honor your father and mother.'"

"Teacher," he declared, "all these I have kept since I was a boy."

Jesus looked at him and loved him. "One thing you lack," he said. "Go, sell everything you have and give to the poor, and you will have treasure in heaven. Then come, follow me."

At this the man's face fell. He went away sad, because he had great wealth.

Jesus looked around and said to his disciples, "How hard it is for the rich to enter the kingdom of God!"

The disciples were amazed at his words. But Jesus said again, "Children, how hard it is to enter the kingdom of God! It is easier for a camel to go through the eye of a needle than for a rich man to enter the kingdom of God."

The disciples were even more amazed, and said to each other, "Who then can be saved?"

Jesus looked at them and said, "With man this is impossible, but not with God; all things are possible with God."

Peter said to him, "We have left everything to follow you!"

"I tell you the truth," Jesus replied, "no one who has left home or brothers or sisters or mother or father or children or fields for me and the gospel will fail to receive a hundred times as much in this present age (homes, brothers, sisters, mothers, children and fields—and with them, persecutions) and in the age to come, eternal life. But many who are first will be last, and the last first." (Mark 10:17-31)

Reflect:

It's a really good question actually. One that each and every one of us, if we're completely honest, has had run through our minds a time or two. *What do I have to do to get to heaven?* What's it really going to take to get me in?

Maybe he was looking for a minimum requirement, or maybe he was hoping for a response that indicated he (being healthy, wealthy, and wise) was already in, I'm not sure. But I do know that he did not get the answer he expected. I really believe that deep in his own heart and soul he was thinking that surely he, of all people, was going to be okay. I mean if he wasn't in, who was? Even the disciples were thinking that. But the ways and the words of God are never so predictable.

Jesus looks deeply into the young man's heart and quickly puts his finger and on the real issue. He immediately identifies the main area of belief that needs to be brought to light and dealt with before faith could become a real possibility for this young, wealthy, and powerful man.

"What's it going to take? Everything! Everything you've got. I want it all." And that is what Jesus requires of each of us as well. Simply put, there's no such thing as coming to Jesus half way. It's all or nothing. There is no minimum investment, no minimum requirement. He wants all of us—all of our heart, all our life, all of our attention, and all of our affection. He wants to be our treasure, not one of many treasures.

He calls us, as he did the rich young ruler, to leave everything behind and come and follow him. This rich man walked away sad, unwilling to allow Jesus to be his all. What is about you?

Respond:
The main issue of the rich young man's heart was his wealth, what is yours? What is your treasure? How does it keep you from totally following Jesus? What is your response today as Jesus says, "Come and follow me?" Write about it in your journal.

Rest:
Jesus is our treasure and we are his. Rest in this truth today.

Forty-Nine

Read:
They were on their way up to Jerusalem, with Jesus leading the way, and the disciples were astonished, while those who followed were afraid. Again he took the Twelve aside and told them what was going to happen to him. "We are going up to Jerusalem," he said, "and the Son of Man will be betrayed to the chief priests and teachers of the law. They will condemn him to death and will hand him over to the Gentiles, who will mock him and spit on him, flog him and kill him. Three days later he will rise." (Mark 10:32-34)

Reflect:
Jesus and his friends now turn toward Jerusalem...*with Jesus leading the way.* Is that not amazing? After all, he clearly knows *all* that stands before him. He knows specifically *all* that the hours and days ahead will hold for him. And yet there he is, *leading the way,* walking right into suffering and sacrifice and death.

His walk is intentional and purposeful as he moves toward the place and the time where his entire mission will come to fruition. After all, this is the very reason he had come to earth to begin with, and now the time for it all to be fulfilled was drawing near.

The disciples weren't totally in the dark, they knew enough from both the anger and the frustration of the Jews that Jesus was heading right into the teeth of a volatile situation. They had to be astonished that he would have the courage and the passion to do such a thing, but they still did not yet fully understand the total extent of his mission.

So as they are traveling, Jesus pulls them aside to try once again to help them understand what they are really walking into. They had a completely different concept of what the word *Messiah* meant—a different vision and different expectations of how this all would play out. They were envisioning a Messiah that was coming to conquer and overthrow. Little did they know what the conquering and overthrowing would look like.

So Jesus tries to help them begin to see things differently, to see things from his point of view. He needs them to begin to see with his eyes, lest the days ahead throw them into doubt and confusion and despair. Because when they are finally able to see with the eyes of Jesus, suddenly their lives and their role and their mission in the world would begin to come into much sharper focus.

Respond:
How is Jesus calling you to join him in his mission? In what ways is He leading you to follow him toward Jerusalem?

Rest:
Rest in his great love for you, love that would cause him to walk purposefully and intentionally towards his suffering and death.

Fifty

Read:
Then James and John, the sons of Zebedee, came to him. "Teacher," they said, "we want you to do for us whatever we ask."

"What do you want me to do for you?" he asked.

They replied, "Let one of us sit at your right and the other at your left in your glory."

"You don't know what you are asking," Jesus said. "Can you drink the cup I drink or be baptized with the baptism I am baptized with?"

"We can," they answered. Jesus said to them, "You will drink the cup I drink and be baptized with the baptism I am baptized with, but to sit at my right or left is not for me to grant. These places belong to those for whom they have been prepared."

When the ten heard about this, they became indignant with James and John. Jesus called them together and said, "You know that those who are regarded as rulers of the Gentiles lord it over them, and their high officials exercise authority over them. Not so with you. Instead, whoever wants to become great among you must be your servant, and whoever wants to be first must be slave of all. For even the Son of Man did not come to be served, but to serve, and to give his life as a ransom for many." (Mark 10:35-45)

Reflect:
They say that *timing is everything*, be it good or be it bad. That certainly seems to be the case with the disciples, who more often than not tend to possess the bad rather than the good. In fact, twice in the last three chapters, directly after Jesus pours out his heart and tries to explain his mission, his passion, and his upcoming sacrifice, their insecurities get the best of them. And unfortunately, even this won't be the last time. It will happen again on the night of his suffering and death, in the upper room, just moments after he washes their feet and shares with them his body and blood (Luke 22:24).

On this occasion James and John, the sons of Zebedee, are the culprits. Just as Jesus is telling them about the selfless nature of his kingdom and his mission, their selfishness rears its ugly head. They brazenly come forward and ask Jesus for a special favor. They ask him for the seats of greatest honor in the coming kingdom. And as soon as they had asked the question, Jesus must have realized that he had a lot more work to do. Somehow they still didn't get it. They still didn't really *see*. They still believed that this whole journey was about them.

And we are exactly the same. We are just like Zebedee's sons. In fact, if we are honest, we have to admit that the true state of our hearts is a complete mess. We too are self-consumed and self-centered; filled with self-importance, self-preservation and self-protection. Self, self, self. Which is exactly what Jesus is trying to address in the question that follows, *"Can you drink the cup I drink or be baptized with the baptism I am baptized with?"*

He, once again, is trying patiently to explain the difference between the world's perspective and that of the kingdom. Jesus desperately wants them see the truth as he tries to challenge and transform their whole way of thinking; attempting to expose their true beliefs and call them away from *self* to something much bigger.

Respond:
What is you first response to Jesus' words? What do they do within you? Are you apt to try and strengthen and fortify the *self* rather than surrendering and/or denying it? Are you more prone to seeking greatness or seeking to be a servant? This week, how will you consciously choose to make yourself a servant?

Rest:
Rest in your total surrender to God's care and God's will.

Fifty-One

Read:

Then they came to Jericho. As Jesus and his disciples, together with a large crowd, were leaving the city, a blind man, Bartimaeus (that is, the Son of Timaeus), was sitting by the roadside begging. When he heard that it was Jesus of Nazareth, he began to shout, "Jesus, Son of David, have mercy on me!"

Many rebuked him and told him to be quiet, but he shouted all the more, "Son of David, have mercy on me!"

Jesus stopped and said, "Call him." So they called to the blind man, "Cheer up! On your feet! He's calling you." Throwing his cloak aside, he jumped to his feet and came to Jesus.

"What do you want me to do for you?" Jesus asked him.

The blind man said, "Rabbi, I want to see."

"Go," said Jesus, "your faith has healed you." Immediately he received his sight and followed Jesus along the road. (Mark 10:46-52)

Reflect:

What a question! Of all the things He could've asked, of all the things that He could've said, somehow Jesus knew that these were the words Bartimaeus most needed to hear. What do you want me to do for you? It is a question that cuts right to the heart of the matter.

This one question shows exactly what Bartimaeus truly believes will make his life worth living. This one question holds the key to the chains that have bound him for so many years. And the answer Bartimaeus gives to this one little question is absolutely beautiful, "Rabbi, I want to see...Jesus, what I need most is to have my eyes opened." And indeed they were...and his life was never the same again.

Do you think he could do the same for anyone who asked? Even for you and me? If Jesus turned to you right now and asked you the exact same question, what would your answer be?

Respond:

Sit for a few moments in silence and allow yourself to listen deeply. Listen deeply as Jesus asks you the question, "What do you want me to do for you?" What is your answer?

Rest:

Feel his hands upon that one place in your heart and soul where you are most in need of healing. Rest for a few minutes in his healing touch.

Fifty-Two

Read:

As they approached Jerusalem and came to Bethphage and Bethany at the Mount of Olives, Jesus sent two of his disciples, saying to them, "Go to the village ahead of you, and just as you enter it, you will find a colt tied there, which no one has ever ridden. Untie it and bring it here. If anyone asks you, 'Why are you doing this?' say, 'The Lord needs it and will send it back here shortly.'"

They went and found a colt outside in the street, tied at a doorway. As they untied it, some people standing there asked, "What are you doing, untying that colt?" They answered as Jesus had told them to, and the people let them go. When they brought the colt to Jesus and threw their cloaks over it, he sat on it. Many people spread their cloaks on the road, while others spread branches they had cut in the fields. Those who went ahead and those who followed shouted,

"Hosanna!"
"Blessed is he who comes in the name of the Lord!"
"Blessed is the coming kingdom of our father David!"
"Hosanna in the highest heaven!" (Mark 11:1-10)

Reflect:

Willingness is such an essential ingredient in the life of faith. It involves absolute trust and total surrender; requiring the release our will and our agenda for the sake of God's will and God's way. Ultimately willingness involves a submission to following his lead, even if it takes us to places we'd rather not go.

To be willing is to be obedient to his words and his call. To be willing is to let his Spirit have its way with us. To be willing is to stop being consumed with ourselves and start being consumed with God—his desires, his purposes, and his work. To be willing means to love him above all else.

Jesus is the ultimate model of willingness. Never was this on display more clearly than when he made his entrance into Jerusalem. In this one act Jesus shows how he fully embraces God's will, God's plan, and God's way, regardless of the cost. It is the ultimate example of a willing heart—laying aside his own desires in order to accomplish the desires of his Father.

In the days and hours ahead he would be called upon to sacrifice, to suffer, and to die—showing himself willing to even endure taunts and jeers and abuse, accusations and hostility and violence, anguish and desolation and unspeakable loneliness.

As Jesus climbed up on the back of the colt and began his long, slow ride into town, you just have to wonder what must have been going through his mind. What was he thinking as the crowd began to swell and the people began to shout and cheer and spread their coats and their palm branches on the road? What must he have been feeling as the people shouted the word *Hosanna (which means Save!)*, yet had no idea how this would be accomplished or what great price it would come at?

For years and years they had read about, and waited upon, this very moment (Zechariah 6:6). They were all familiar with what the Scriptures had to say about the coming of the Messiah, yet they still didn't really understand. They were still hoping for a Messiah that was coming to put them in power and deliver them from their oppressors (the Romans). They weren't really interested in God's will at all; they were only interested in their own. They were not willing. They were willful; and there is a huge difference between the two.

Being *willing*, as we have seen, involves a surrender of our will in favor of God's will. Being *willful*, however, involves being *full* of our own *will*. Being willful makes us unwilling—unwilling to let God be God, unwilling to let him call the shots, unwilling to let him come in his own time and in his own way and on his own terms.

The crowds that were lining the streets were so consumed with their own needs and so full of their own desires that they could not (or would not) see what was right before them. It must've been strange indeed for Jesus to know that the very people that were chanting *Hosanna* on this day would be the ones that would shout *Crucify him* in the days and hours to come. And even though he fully knew all of that, he was still *willing*. Aren't you glad he was?

Respond:
What word best describes your life and heart right now *willing* or *willful*? When you hear the word *willing* what does it do inside of you? Are you *willing*? Where are you *willing*? Where are you *willful*? What is God saying to you in all of this?

Rest:
Spend a few minutes in silence before God. As you are with him, open your hands before him, showing him your willingness, whatever that may mean. Rest in his willingness to be with you.

Fifty-Three

Read:
Jesus entered Jerusalem and went into the temple courts. He looked around at everything, but since it was already late, he went out to Bethany with the Twelve.

The next day as they were leaving Bethany, Jesus was hungry. Seeing in the distance a fig tree in leaf, he went to find out if it had any fruit. When he reached it, he found nothing but leaves, because it was not the season for figs. Then he said to the tree, "May no one ever eat fruit from you again." And his disciples heard him say it.

On reaching Jerusalem, Jesus entered the temple courts and began driving out those who were buying and selling there. He overturned the tables of the money changers and the benches of those selling doves, and would not allow anyone to carry merchandise through the temple courts. And as he taught them, he said, "Is it not written: 'My house will be called a house of prayer for all nations'? But you have made it 'a den of robbers.'"

The chief priests and the teachers of the law heard this and began looking for a way to kill him, for they feared him, because the whole crowd was amazed at his teaching.

When evening came, Jesus and his disciples went out of the city.

In the morning, as they went along, they saw the fig tree withered from the roots. Peter remembered and said to Jesus, "Rabbi, look! The fig tree you cursed has withered!"

"Have faith in God," Jesus answered. "Truly I tell you, if anyone says to this mountain, 'Go, throw yourself into the sea,' and does not doubt in their heart but believes that what they say will happen, it will be done for them. Therefore I tell you, whatever you ask for in prayer, believe that you have received it, and it will be yours. And when you stand praying, if you hold anything against anyone, forgive them, so that your Father in heaven may forgive you your sins." (Mark 11:11-26)

Reflect:

At one point or another most of us have probably heard the phrase "actions speak louder than words." And though it is an age-old expression, it is one that couldn't be more true. The fact of the matter is that if you want to see what someone really believes, just watch what they do. If you want to see what they value most, what they hold as important, watch how they spend their time. If you want to know what someone really loves, watch the direction their feet start to move the first time they get the chance.

That is certainly true of Jesus. The very first thing he does when he arrives in Jerusalem is go straight to the temple. It tells us so much about him: about his heart, about his priorities, and about his affections. His deep love for the Father is the driving force behind his life. He just can't stay away from the temple—it is his Father's house and where he most wants to be. It is the very center of his life.

But on this occasion, it is not the most joyful trip to the temple he has ever made. That's because as Jesus enters the temple on this particular occasion and looks around at all that is going on, what he sees breaks his heart. What he sees is not the temple as it was created to be—the place for all people to offer themselves to God—but the temple as it had become; the place for the powerful to profit off of the poor in the name of religion. Can you imagine the hurt he must've felt, and the pain? Can you imagine the frustration? Here he is, coming home to his Father's house, and the first thing he runs into is a bunch of crooks—people caring neither for the temple nor the Father, but only for themselves.

What is really amazing about the situation is that instead of a knee-jerk reaction to it all—hastily responding to what he has seen and heard—after carefully looking around he retreats to Bethany with his friends to reflect on it all. His response would come alright, but it would come in a thoughtful, intentional, and prayerful manner rather than one based solely on emotion or frustration.

So the next day he sets out on his return. And as he and his friends travel to the temple, he passes a fig tree. Jesus is hungry and goes over to the tree looking for fruit, but there is no fruit to be found—for it wasn't the season for figs. And after a night of reflecting on the fruitlessness he saw in the temple the day before, Jesus (as he always does) decides to take this opportunity as a teachable moment for his disciples. He curses the tree for bearing no fruit and says *May no one ever eat from you again.*

But what, exactly, is the lesson he is trying to teach? I mean, after all, it wasn't the season for figs, so why blame the poor fig tree? Isn't it funny that we are so quick to try and defend a tree? But I think that's our first response because the whole scene makes us really uncomfortable. It makes us uneasy. Why? Maybe because it seems like a really hard lesson he's trying to teach—God will not tolerate fruitlessness. Even if we think we have good and valid excuses for why there is no fruit; in God's eyes there is no excuse—not with a tree and certainly not with a people.

So after addressing a fruitless tree he continues on to the temple to address a fruitless people. And as he arrives, he enters the temple and begins to turn everything upside down: driving out those buying and selling, overturning the tables of the moneychangers, knocking over the benches of those selling doves.

Had all of these people grown so cold to God, and the things of God, that they were actually trying to cheat (and take advantage of) the very people who were coming to genuinely seek Him? And those who were selling doves (the poor man's sacrifice) were the worst of all—actually trying to cheat the poorest of the poor. All of this not only broke Jesus' heart, but it made him mad. He just couldn't stand by and watch—he wouldn't. He had to address it all; had to do something about the injustice.

And what about the disciples? What were they doing while all of this was going on? Do you think they were surprised? Do you imagine that they were standing there open-mouthed and amazed? Or do you think they were enjoying it? Were they joining in? Or could they have been terrified, afraid of the ramifications of all that was happening before their very eyes? Do you think they understood all that was going on or do you think they were confused? Did they comprehend the connection between the tree and the temple? What about later when they saw the tree was *withered from the roots*? What did they think and feel then? And what do you think they thought of what Jesus said to them after they saw the fate of the fig tree? Was this all a lesson about faith? Or about prayer? Or was it a lesson about fruitlessness and fruitfulness?

What is God saying to you about it all?

Respond:
What does the *tree of your life* look like right now? Where do you see fruit? Where is there fruitlessness? Draw a picture of that tree in your journal, taking time to recognize both areas. What do you notice? What is God saying to you about the things you have noticed?

Rest:
Take a few minutes and rest in Jesus, the source of all life, the true vine who alone can make all things fruitful.

Fifty-Four

Read:
They arrived again in Jerusalem, and while Jesus was walking in the temple courts, the chief priests, the teachers of the law and the elders came to him. "By what authority are you doing these things?" they asked. "And who gave you authority to do this?"

Jesus replied, "I will ask you one question. Answer me, and I will tell you by what authority I am doing these things. John's baptism—was it from heaven, or of human origin? Tell me!"

They discussed it among themselves and said, "If we say, 'From heaven,' he will ask, 'Then why didn't you believe him?' But if we say, 'Of human origin' ..." (They feared the people, for everyone held that John really was a prophet.)

So they answered Jesus, "We don't know."

Jesus said, "Neither will I tell you by what authority I am doing these things." (Mark 11:27-33)

Reflect:
Jesus had consistently called their hearts into question. He had even gone as far as to turn over their tables and scatter their enterprises, literally as well as figuratively. He had "upset the apple cart;" threatening their entire religious system, as well as their whole way of life. His words and actions endangered both their position and their reputation, so much so that they were actually looking for ways to kill him.

The religious leaders just couldn't allow him to gain any more momentum, so they went on the offensive. They decided to attack by calling him, and his actions, into question. Their strategy was to ask Jesus by what authority he did all of these things. Who was it that gave him the right, and the power, to make such statements and to do such things? Who was he to sit in judgment of them?

Maybe they were asking the question for themselves and maybe they were asking the question for the sake of those who were listening—in hopes that hearing his answer might begin to change the popular sentiment. Whatever the reason, they had to find a way to turn the people against him; which would not be an easy task. The bottom line was that they were trying to trap him into saying something that could be used against him. Just imagine, trying to trap God; trying to trick him into a mistake that you could use to your advantage.

Jesus, however, didn't fall for their trick. He instead, did what he did so often, and answered their question with a question. Whenever you answer a question with a question, especially a really good one, it puts the ball squarely back in the other person's court. Instead of trying to give an answer to a manipulative, no-win question, he turns the tables back on them. It was as if they were playing a game of verbal chess and now Jesus had them in checkmate.

The next move was theirs, but there was absolutely no move to make. So they simply refused to answer; which played right into Jesus' hands. It allowed him the freedom to play the same game, to do the very same thing back at them. No matter how hard they tried, they just couldn't pin him down.

We all play similar games with God from time to time don't we? We try to manipulate him into giving us what we want. We try to say just the right words and do just the right things and not really show our hand, hoping God will not figure out our true intentions—giving us the result we are really looking for. It is ridiculous when you think about it; yet we continue to play the games nonetheless.

God, however, will not be manipulated. He is not a game player—he is God. He cannot be trapped; he cannot be tricked, he cannot be "played," no matter how hard we try and no matter how clever we think we are.

Respond:
What kind of games do you play with God? In what ways do you try to manipulate him? Ask him to show you your manipulative and demanding patterns. Give them all to him and ask him for the strength, the power, and the grace to change your ways.

Rest:
Just rest in God's love and acceptance this day, no matter how demanding and manipulative you may be.

Fifty-Five

Read:
Jesus then began to speak to them in parables: "A man planted a vineyard. He put a wall around it, dug a pit for the winepress and built a watchtower. Then he rented the vineyard to some farmers and moved to another place. At harvest time he sent a servant to the tenants to collect from them some of the fruit of the vineyard. But they seized him, beat him and sent him away empty-handed. Then he sent another servant to them; they struck this man on the head and treated him shamefully. He sent still another, and that one they killed. He sent many others; some of them they beat, others they killed.

"He had one left to send, a son, whom he loved. He sent him last of all, saying, 'They will respect my son.'

"But the tenants said to one another, 'This is the heir. Come, let's kill him, and the inheritance will be ours.' So they took him and killed him, and threw him out of the vineyard.

"What then will the owner of the vineyard do? He will come and kill those tenants and give the vineyard to others. Haven't you read this passage of Scripture:

"'The stone the builders rejected
has become the cornerstone;
the Lord has done this,
and it is marvelous in our eyes'?"

Then the chief priests, the teachers of the law and the elders looked for a way to arrest him because they knew he had spoken the parable against them. But they were afraid of the crowd; so they left him and went away. (Mark 12:1-12)

Reflect:
Jesus is in the temple courts once again, and people have gathered around from everywhere—people filled with curiosity, filled with longing, desperate for hope. They were people that were leaning forward, standing on tiptoe, waiting and yearning just to hear a word from his lips or to see a miracle from his hands. And as the crowds grew, so did their anticipation. They were hungry to hear whatever he might have to say. So Jesus simply began to tell them stories.

He told stories about life, and faith, and God. He told stories about brothers, and fathers, and sons; about farmers, and workers, and landowners; about priests, and widows, and Samaritans. But in every case, he told stories ultimately about God—about His character, His heart, and His kingdom.

These stories serve as windows into the world of the Spirit, offering all people access to the mysteries of God. They are stories set in familiar settings, painted in familiar images, and spoken in a familiar language—in order to be understandable to all. They are stories offering a point of entry—a doorway. Stories in which each character offers a doorway, not only into the mind and heart of God, but also into a deeper understanding of ourselves and where we stand in relation to Him.

So as we read these stories (parables), maybe the very best thing we can _do_ is to step into the shoes of each of the characters and see what each one has to say to us—what they have to teach us. And maybe, as we read, the best thing we can _ask_ is, "Where do I see myself in this story?" And maybe, just maybe, through this _doing_ and through this _asking,_ God will speak to us in ways we have never imagined before.

Respond:
Where do you see yourself in the story of the farmers and the vineyard owner? What is each character like? What does each character have to say to you? What is God saying to you through this story?

Rest:
Rest in the love of a God who loves you enough to send his son to die for you.

Fifty-Six

Read:
Later they sent some of the Pharisees and Herodians to Jesus to catch him in his words. They came to him and said, "Teacher, we know that you are a man of integrity. You aren't swayed by others, because you pay no attention to who they are; but you teach the way of God in accordance with the truth. Is it right to pay the imperial tax to Caesar or not? Should we pay or shouldn't we?"

But Jesus knew their hypocrisy. "Why are you trying to trap me?" he asked. "Bring me a denarius and let me look at it." They brought the coin, and he asked them, "Whose image is this? And whose inscription?"

"Caesar's," they replied.

Then Jesus said to them, "Give back to Caesar what is Caesar's and to God what is God's."

And they were amazed at him. (Mark 12:13-17)

Reflect:
But Jesus knew their hypocrisy…

> hyp·o·crite [hip-_uh_-crit] 1. A person who pretends to have virtues, moral or religious beliefs, principles, etc., that he or she does not actually possess, esp. a person whose actions belie stated beliefs.

In Greek, the *hupocritēs* were the actors on the stage, playing a role. So when Mark tells us that Jesus knew their hypocrisy, it means that he knew the truth. He knew that the religious leaders of Israel were only pretending; that deep inside they had no real life with God. And while they might be able to fool and intimidate the average person, they could neither fool, nor intimidate him. He knew the truth, and the truth was that they didn't care for God, or the people of God—they only cared for themselves.

Jesus always sees into the heart, which is both a wonderful and a terrifying thing. For if *Jesus knew their hypocrisy*, Jesus knows our hypocrisy. Jesus knows my hypocrisy. He knows when I am not being real. Or worse, he knows when I am purposefully being false. He knows when I am lying and he knows when I'm just trying to fake it. He cannot and will not be fooled. What he longs for most is for us to be real with him, and with each other, because he will always be real with us.

Respond:
Where are you acting? Where are you faking it? Where are you living falsely? With people? With God? What would it look like to live a more genuine life? Where do you need to stop pretending and open your life up to God? Where do you need to open your life up to another person and let someone see what's really there? Do that with someone you know and trust this week. I think you will find that real openness and vulnerability brings life, healing, and wholeness.

Rest:
Spend a few minutes resting in God, who knows you best and loves you most.

Fifty-Seven

Read:
Then the Sadducees, who say there is no resurrection, came to him with a question. "Teacher," they said, "Moses wrote for us that if a man's brother dies and leaves a wife but no children, the man must marry the widow and raise up offspring for his brother. Now there were seven brothers. The first one married and died without leaving any children. The second one married the widow, but he also died, leaving no child. It was the same with the third. In fact, none of the seven left any children. Last of all, the woman died too. At the resurrection whose wife will she be, since the seven were married to her?"

Jesus replied, "Are you not in error because you do not know the Scriptures or the power of God? When the dead rise, they will neither marry nor be given in marriage; they will be like the angels in heaven. Now about the dead rising—have you not read in the Book of Moses, in the

account of the burning bush, how God said to him, 'I am the God of
Abraham, the God of Isaac, and the God of Jacob'? He is not the God of
the dead, but of the living. You are badly mistaken!" (Mark 12:18-27)

Reflect:
Marriage is a great gift. And it was always intended to be a window, a
beautiful picture of God's desire for intimacy with his people. It is a
physical and tangible relationship which is given to reveal to us a deep
mystery; that God is our ultimate lover and that the intimate love shared
between a husband and a wife is just a taste of what God most longs for
with each of us.

The Sadducees didn't understand this, or many other things about
Jesus for that matter. So when they come to him with their question about
marriage and the resurrection, they are really exposing how little they know
about either of the subjects; because ultimately man was made to be
"married to God."

So, in the life to come, there will be no marriage because each of us will
finally have been joined in union forever with our Beloved Spouse, Jesus.
The book of Revelation describes it so beautifully when it paints a portrait
of the end times being a wedding feast; the wedding feast of the Lamb
(Jesus) and his beautiful bride (us).

I know it is hard for us, especially us men, to imagine ourselves as a
beautiful bride, but that is indeed what we are. In fact, the book of Isaiah
(62:5) tells us that *as a bridegroom rejoices over his bride, so our God*
rejoices over us. Can you imagine that God looks at us the same way that
a groom looks at his bride as the doors open and she walks down the
aisle? I've had the privilege of seeing that look on many occasions as I
have performed weddings. It is a look of sheer delight. It is a look of
awestruck wonder. It is a look of overwhelming love and affection. It is a
look of deep desire. A look more filled with love there may never be.

The fact is that we are loved more passionately, more deeply, and more
intimately than we could ever imagine. How sad that the Sadducees
missed all of that. Hopefully you and I won't.

Respond:
Think back to the weddings you have been to. What was the look on the
grooms face? What was his response to seeing his beautiful bride coming
down the aisle to meet him? Try and imagine that look of love on the face
of God...directed at you. What is the look in his eyes? What does that tell
you about the love in his heart? What is his reaction to your coming to
meet him? Draw or write about what you see.

Rest:
A wise saint once told me that "prayer is the silent embrace of two lovers."
Rest now in the embrace of your Beloved Spouse.

Fifty-Eight

Read:

One of the teachers of the law came and heard them debating. Noticing that Jesus had given them a good answer, he asked him, "Of all the commandments, which is the most important?"

"The most important one," answered Jesus, "is this: 'Hear, O Israel: The Lord our God, the Lord is one. Love the Lord your God with all your heart and with all your soul and with all your mind and with all your strength.' The second is this: 'Love your neighbor as yourself.' There is no commandment greater than these."

"Well said, teacher," the man replied. "You are right in saying that God is one and there is no other but him. To love him with all your heart, with all your understanding and with all your strength, and to love your neighbor as yourself is more important than all burnt offerings and sacrifices."

When Jesus saw that he had answered wisely, he said to him, "You are not far from the kingdom of God." And from then on no one dared ask him any more questions. (Mark 12:28-34)

Reflect:

"Of all the commandments, which is the most important?" What an incredible question! It is a question that cuts through all the peripheral issues and goes right to the heart of the matter. *"Of all the great things God has said, what is the greatest?"* It's quite possibly the best [recorded] question anyone ever asked Jesus, because, at its core, it appears to be a question that longs to know the truth, the point, main thing, the very heart of God.

And I guess it should come as no surprise that Jesus' answer to this question has everything to do with love. Love is the point. Love is the main thing. Love is most important—God's great love for us, and our love, in response, for him...and then for one another. These are the three main movements of the spiritual life.

First, we must become convinced that we are deeply, extravagantly, and unconditionally loved by the God who made us; that God calls us his Beloved. Once we have firmly rooted ourselves in that great love we must, in turn, respond to that love by giving him all that we are—*heart, soul, mind and strength*—turning to him and calling him our Beloved as well. And finally, as a result of us being his beloved, and he being our beloved, we turn, in love, toward one another. That is God's design.

Respond:

Do you know that God calls you his Beloved? Are you able to call him your Beloved as well? Write down what it means to love him with all your heart...with all your soul...with all your mind...with all your strength.

Rest:
Rest in God's immense love for you...and your love for him in return.

Fifty-Nine

Read:
While Jesus was teaching in the temple courts, he asked, "Why do the teachers of the law say that the Messiah is the son of David? David himself, speaking by the Holy Spirit, declared:

"'The Lord said to my Lord:
"Sit at my right hand
until I put your enemies
under your feet."'

David himself calls him 'Lord.' How then can he be his son?"
The large crowd listened to him with delight. (Mark 12:35-37)

Reflect:
They were always planning and scheming, relentless in their attempts to trap Jesus in his words. They were constantly trying to gain an advantage in the ongoing debate; every discussion holding a hidden snare, every question containing a hook, each trying to lure him to take the bait. It had to be getting old.

So this time Jesus goes on the offensive. With a playful grin and a mischievous smile Jesus asks them a question for a change; a question that they have absolutely no answer for, a question that exposes both their hearts as well as their flawed logic, but also a question that gives them a hint as to the true nature and identity of the Messiah. And he even uses the very thing they profess to be experts in (the Old Testament) as he make his point—quoting Psalm 110:1 to challenge them with what the scriptures truly teach about the Messiah.

All of the religious leaders knew well that the Messiah was supposed to come from the line of David. This was without dispute. It was also widely held by the experts of the law that Psalm 110 was written about the Messiah. But how could the Messiah be both David's son and David's Lord at the same time? None of them had an answer for this question, they were completely stumped. Maybe for the first time in their lives they were actually at a loss for words...and the crowds were delighted.

It is the answer to this rather odd question that holds the key to understanding both Jesus' identity and his authority. For the only way it could be possible for someone to be both son and Lord is if he were both God and man at the same time; which is exactly what Jesus is—the God-man. This is where His authority came from; and this is what the religious leaders refused to acknowledge.

Respond:
Jesus' question was meant to be disruptive in the minds and hearts of his listeners. He was attempting to rearrange their thoughts and beliefs about him. How has Jesus been disruptive in your life? How has he tried to rearrange your thoughts and beliefs about him in order to show you who he really is?

Rest:
Simply rest in the presence of Jesus, who is bigger than all of our questions.

Sixty

Read:
As he taught, Jesus said, "Watch out for the teachers of the law. They like to walk around in flowing robes and be greeted with respect in the marketplaces, and have the most important seats in the synagogues and the places of honor at banquets. They devour widows' houses and for a show make lengthy prayers. These men will be punished most severely." (Mark 12:38-40)

Reflect:
Watch out. Although Jesus is referring to the teachers of the law in this passage, his warning is for us all. After all, who doesn't like being greeted with respect? Which of us doesn't want the most important seats at anything, much less at the place of worship? Who among us wouldn't desire the places of honor at banquets? These are things we all secretly (and in some cases not so secretly) strive for. But, as Jesus warns, they are not things worthy of his kingdom; not things to be pursued or sought after.

The focus of the kingdom is much different than this. The kingdom of God is about caring for the poor and the widows, not devouring them for personal gain. The kingdom of God is about the gut wrenchingly honest prayers of God's people offered to him alone in the secret places of our hearts, not the lengthy babblings of the self-seeking, offered only for show. Jesus was very clear, both here and in the book of Mathew, that when we do our "acts of faith" so that they might be seen by others, we don't really do "acts of faith" at all, but only acts of self-seeking indulgence.

So any time we are tempted to do something in order to be seen or to be honored or to be viewed as important by others, we should watch out.

Because when we are pursuing these things we are acting more like the opponents of the kingdom than we are like the citizens of the kingdom.

Respond:
In what ways are you tempted to do things to be *seen* or *honored* or considered *important*? How is Jesus' warning to *watch out* for you?

Rest:
Rest for a few minutes in the hidden presence of our unseen, but ever-present, God.

Sixty-One

Read:
Jesus sat down opposite the place where the offerings were put and watched the crowd putting their money into the temple treasury. Many rich people threw in large amounts. But a poor widow came and put in two very small copper coins, worth only a few cents.
Calling his disciples to him, Jesus said, "Truly I tell you, this poor widow has put more into the treasury than all the others. They all gave out of their wealth; but she, out of her poverty, put in everything—all she had to live on." (Mark 12:41-44)

Reflect:
What do you think Jesus was really paying attention to as he *sat down opposite the place where the offerings were put and watched the crowd putting their money into the temple treasury*? The answer to this question will tell you a significant amount about what you believe to be most true about him. What, exactly, was it that he was watching for?

Was he looking more at how much the people gave or at the spirit with which they gave it? Was he more concerned with amount or with attitude? And what do you think his eyes were most focused on: their hands, their posture, their faces, their eyes?

The Old Testament tells us that *"The eyes of the Lord search the whole earth in order to strengthen those whose hearts are fully committed to him"* (2 Chronicles 16:9). So maybe what his eyes were most focused on were their hearts; having that incredible ability, somehow, to look past their outward appearance and focus directly on their inner thoughts, motives, and attitudes. And what he discovered was one heart that was totally given to him—that of a poor widow—for she gave *everything she had*.

It's a question each of us asks ourselves from time to time, if we are completely honest. *How much will I give?* Or maybe the better question would be, *how much will I keep?* Do we ask these questions because, when it gets right down to it, we are really looking for something that won't cost us too much? It seems that we either want to give out of our wealth—so that it will not really cost us very much personally—or we are looking for some kind of minimum requirement; looking for how little I can give and still be okay.

And it's not just money, we do that with everything; particularly with whatever is most valuable to each of us—our treasure (Matthew 6:21) so to speak. How much do I give? How much of my time, or my talents, or my career, or my future, or my attention, or my agenda, or my control do I give him?

And, of course, the answer is *all of it*. That is the incredible mystery of the kingdom; that the only way to find true life and joy and peace is to give it *all* to him. We must be willing to give him *all* our hearts—just as the poor widow did. There is no other way, no matter how hard we try to convince ourselves otherwise—life with Jesus requires it *all*.

Respond:
Draw a picture of your heart. What color, and shape, and state best describe the real condition of your heart right now? What lies within it? What areas does God have free reign of? And what areas are you still holding out or holding back?

Rest:
Offer your heart to your Heavenly Father, just as it is; knowing that he loves you deeply and will care for it tenderly. He is worthy of your complete and total trust—even with your heart.

Sixty-Two

Read:
As Jesus was leaving the temple, one of his disciples said to him, "Look, Teacher! What massive stones! What magnificent buildings!"

"Do you see all these great buildings?" replied Jesus. "Not one stone here will be left on another; every one will be thrown down." (Mark 13:1-2)

Reflect:
The temple in Jerusalem was a magnificent structure. It was estimated at being around 20 stories tall and was built from stones averaging 100 tons each; with some being as large as 400 tons. It was absolutely massive; one of the most impressive structures ever built by man. No wonder the disciples were filled with awe as they looked at it.

So needless to say they must have been more than a little surprised by Jesus' statement that, at some point in time, *not one stone would be left on another*. For as big and as impressive as the temple was, he wanted them to know that it would not last. One day, like every other creation of man, it would all be destroyed; every last stone would *be thrown down.*

The unavoidable fact is that even the greatest and most impressive things that man can build with his own hands are only temporary. None of them will last…not even one. For only the things of God are eternal.

We would be wise to remember this fact as well; for our heads, like theirs, are constantly being turned by the size of our own achievements and accomplishments—by the works of our own hands. It's what our lives are totally consumed with. We *make* a living, *build a* reputation, *create* a resume, and *make* a name for ourselves—forever putting our trust in our own energy and efforts.

This lesson is truly for us all: no matter how impressive the results, we must always realize that everything, other than the things of God, will eventually come to an end. So why on earth do we work so hard on things which, one-day, will crumble to the ground?

Respond:
What impressive structures are you trying to build in your life? What do they look like? How long will they last? What "works of your hands" are you trusting in? What will happen when it all crumbles to the ground?

Rest:
Rest in God's eternal, unchanging hand.

Sixty-Three

Read:
As Jesus was sitting on the Mount of Olives opposite the temple, Peter, James, John and Andrew asked him privately, "Tell us, when will these things happen? And what will be the sign that they are all about to be fulfilled?"

Jesus said to them: "Watch out that no one deceives you. Many will come in my name, claiming, 'I am he,' and will deceive many. When you hear of wars and rumors of wars, do not be alarmed. Such things must happen, but the end is still to come. Nation will rise against nation, and kingdom against kingdom. There will be earthquakes in various places, and famines. These are the beginning of birth pains.

"You must be on your guard. You will be handed over to the local councils and flogged in the synagogues. On account of me you will stand before governors and kings as witnesses to them. And the gospel must first be preached to all nations. Whenever you are arrested and brought to trial, do not worry beforehand about what to say. Just say whatever is given you at the time, for it is not you speaking, but the Holy Spirit.

"Brother will betray brother to death, and a father his child. Children will rebel against their parents and have them put to death. Everyone will hate you because of me, but the one who stands firm to the end will be saved.

"When you see 'the abomination that causes desolation' standing where it does not belong—let the reader understand—then let those who are in Judea flee to the mountains. Let no one on the housetop go down or enter the house to take anything out. Let no one in the field go back to get their cloak. How dreadful it will be in those days for pregnant women and nursing mothers! Pray that this will not take place in winter, because those will be days of distress unequaled from the beginning, when God created the world, until now—and never to be equaled again.

"If the Lord had not cut short those days, no one would survive. But for the sake of the elect, whom he has chosen, he has shortened them. At that time if anyone says to you, 'Look, here is the Messiah!' or, 'Look, there he is!' do not believe it. For false messiahs and false prophets will appear and perform signs and wonders to deceive, if possible, even the elect. So be on your guard; I have told you everything ahead of time.

"But in those days, following that distress,

"'the sun will be darkened,
  and the moon will not give its light;
  the stars will fall from the sky,
  and the heavenly bodies will be shaken.'

"At that time people will see the Son of Man coming in clouds with great power and glory. And he will send his angels and gather his elect from the four winds, from the ends of the earth to the ends of the heavens.

"Now learn this lesson from the fig tree: As soon as its twigs get tender and its leaves come out, you know that summer is near. Even so, when you see these things happening, you know that it is near, right at the door. Truly I tell you, this generation will certainly not pass away until all these things have happened. Heaven and earth will pass away, but my words will never pass away.

"But about that day or hour no one knows, not even the angels in heaven, nor the Son, but only the Father. Be on guard! Be alert! You do not know when that time will come. It's like a man going away: He leaves his house and puts his servants in charge, each with their assigned task, and tells the one at the door to keep watch.

"Therefore keep watch because you do not know when the owner of the house will come back—whether in the evening, or at midnight, or when the rooster crows, or at dawn. If he comes suddenly, do not let him find you sleeping. What I say to you, I say to everyone: 'Watch!'" (Mark 13:3-37)

Reflect:

The disciples knew their history. They knew that, although it looked like an impossible feat, the temple had already been destroyed once in 587

B.C. And if they could see into the not-so-distant-future they would be able to see that it would happen once again in 70 A.D. So even as big and as impressive as the temple was, they knew it was not totally indestructible.

The disciples also knew their Scriptures. They knew that any talk of the destruction of the temple could point to something that every Jew waited and longed for—*the Day of the Lord*. It was the day when God would finally come down out of heaven, in power, and put an end to the rule of their enemies once and for all. It was the day when all oppression, and all struggle, and all injustice would be completely done away with. Daniel had written all about it, as had Joel, and Amos, and many others. It was a day that every Jew yearned for and constantly watched and waited for any sign of.

It was this eager anticipation that prompted the disciples to ask Jesus two questions: *When will these things happen? And what will be the sign that they are all about to be fulfilled?* Or more specifically, when will the temple be destroyed? And when will the *Day of the Lord* come? And as we listen to His lengthy reply, it is essential for us to clearly remember that he is answering two separate questions.

The problem is that in his response he doesn't clearly indicate which question he is answering at which time. Therefore, it is really difficult to be sure of anything specific, as far as times and places are concerned. My guess is that he did this on purpose. As we have said before, just about everything Jesus did was very intentional and if he meant for us to know the exact times and places of his return, he would have clearly told us and not left us to wonder.

I have a suspicion that this is due to the fact that we have a tendency to try and control everything—even the things of God. And in order to control things, we need to be able to fully understand and explain them. Thus, we try and reduce mystery to formula; to reduce things that are outside our understanding and control to a level that we can get our minds and arms around them.

Jesus knew this well. He knew that our need for control would always stand in the way of our ability to fully trust in and depend on him. For if we can control things, there will never a need to rely on anyone or anything outside ourselves. We become self-sufficient; needing only to trust in and depend on our own reason or resources.

In our relationship with Jesus there must be some amount of faith involved; there has to be some leap; some level of dependence and trust that fully knowing cannot truly allow. There must always be mystery, because mystery leads us to a place that requires faith and trust. Mystery leads to dependence. Mystery opens us up to his Spirit and his leading. All of which is exactly what he wants.

Respond:
Where in your life is God asking you to embrace mystery? How is he asking you to trust in and depend on him?

Rest:
Spend a few minutes fully resting in the God's care. He alone is worthy of your trust.

Sixty-Four

Read:
Now the Passover and the Festival of Unleavened Bread were only two days away, and the chief priests and the teachers of the law were scheming to arrest Jesus secretly and kill him. "But not during the festival," they said, "or the people may riot."

While he was in Bethany, reclining at the table in the home of Simon the Leper, a woman came with an alabaster jar of very expensive perfume, made of pure nard. She broke the jar and poured the perfume on his head.

Some of those present were saying indignantly to one another, "Why this waste of perfume? It could have been sold for more than a year's wages and the money given to the poor." And they rebuked her harshly.

"Leave her alone," said Jesus. "Why are you bothering her? She has done a beautiful thing to me. The poor you will always have with you, and you can help them any time you want. But you will not always have me. She did what she could. She poured perfume on my body beforehand to prepare for my burial. Truly I tell you, wherever the gospel is preached throughout the world, what she has done will also be told, in memory of her." (Mark 14:1-9)

Reflect:
She was just like any other young woman. She longed for the day when she would meet Mr. Right and be swept off her feet into the romance of her life—a romance that was wilder and more passionate than anything she could ever imagine or hope for.

She had painted the picture in her mind in great detail—spending years and years dreaming and imagining exactly what her wedding day would be like. Saving herself for the very day when she would give all of her love and affection—all of her self—to the one she loved more than her very life. On that day she would pour it all out on him, everything she had, with no holding back.

That was until she met Jesus. Meeting him had changed everything. In him she had experienced a love greater and deeper than she could have ever imagined in her wildest dreams. She loved him so much that she felt like her heart would explode within her if she didn't find some way of expressing it.

And so she goes to her room and opens her dowry; those things intended to be saved for her wedding day, to be given to her Beloved. As she rummaged through the contents she came upon it, the most valuable thing she owned. Giving it to him would be the only way she could even begin to express the depths of her love. So she grabbed her jar of perfume and made her way to the feet of Jesus. It was the perfect gift, the most beautiful and most valuable thing she owned.

She brought it in the room, giving it freely and extravagantly to him. She didn't just pour a little out on him, but the whole thing. She poured and poured, upon his head, without restraint. She poured and poured until it was all gone; until the room was filled with the sweet fragrance of her love and affection. It was a costly act to say the least, worth an entire year's wages. But in her mind and in her heart it was worth every bit of it.

You have to wonder, as she emptied the contents of the jar on her Beloved, if somewhere deep within her heart and soul she uttered the ancient words, "I am my Beloved's and his desire is for me." (Song of Songs 7:10 ESV).

Respond:
What would it look like for you to love Jesus like Mary did? What gift of love would you like to pour out on Jesus, your Beloved?

Rest:
A wise saint once told me that prayer is like "the silent embrace of two lovers." Spend a few minutes in that kind of prayer with God, the lover of your soul.

Sixty-Five

Read:
Then Judas Iscariot, one of the Twelve, went to the chief priests to betray Jesus to them. They were delighted to hear this and promised to give him money. So he watched for an opportunity to hand him over. (Mark 14:10-11)

Reflect:
What a contrast. On the one hand, Mary pours out her love and affection upon Jesus in a beautiful way; giving him absolutely all she has to give. And on the other hand Judas, the one that complained about Mary's extravagance, does the exact opposite. He takes. Judas betrays his friend into the hands of the very people that were trying to kill him, in order to further his own purposes.

At best, he was trying to hasten the coming of the kingdom of God so he could begin his reign with Jesus. And at worst, he was just trying to make a quick buck at the great expense of a dear friend. Either way his chief concern was himself.

These two friends of Jesus present us with the simplicity and the clarity of the choice we have before us each day. Mary gives herself for the love of Jesus and Judas gives Jesus for the love of self. The bottom line is that, in all we do, we can choose to love Jesus or we can choose to love self. It's that simple. Those are really the only two choices before us. We are either like Mary or we are like Judas. Which is it?

Respond:
In your journal, make a list of the ways you are like Mary and the ways you are like Judas. Offer that list to God, in prayer, and ask him to help you grow in your love for Him and to die in your love for self.

Rest:
Spend a few minutes just being with God in love.

Sixty-Six

Read:
On the first day of the Festival of Unleavened Bread, when it was customary to sacrifice the Passover lamb, Jesus' disciples asked him, "Where do you want us to go and make preparations for you to eat the Passover?"

So he sent two of his disciples, telling them, "Go into the city, and a man carrying a jar of water will meet you. Follow him. Say to the owner of the house he enters, 'The Teacher asks: Where is my guest room, where I may eat the Passover with my disciples?' He will show you a large room upstairs, furnished and ready. Make preparations for us there."

The disciples left, went into the city and found things just as Jesus had told them. So they prepared the Passover. (Mark 14:12-16)

Reflect:
Who doesn't love the holidays? They are a time to celebrate, honor, and remember; to take a break from the normal routine, whatever that may be—work, school, duties, obligations, etc. And they are usually a time filled with enjoyable people, places, and things: family and friends, laughter and love, parties and meals, events and festivities; and maybe even a parade or two.

For every Jew it was the holiday season. It was the time of year when entire families would travel up to Jerusalem, singing songs of God's great love and faithfulness, of His help and deliverance. These songs of worship came right out of their prayer book—the Psalms (120-134)—and served as companions and guides for the journey.

Each and every feast was set in place by God to help his people remember and celebrate something very specific about him and his dealings with them throughout their history. The Passover was one of these feasts. It was the time of year when all of Israel celebrated God's deliverance from the hand of the Egyptians. That wonderful and terrible night when the Lord God "passed through Egypt and struck down every firstborn male—both men and animals" from any home that was not protected by the blood of the Passover Lamb spread on the sides and tops of the doorframes. So each year, as they came to Jerusalem and sacrificed their very own Passover lamb, it was a vivid reminder of God's passing over them.

The Feast of Unleavened Bread began after the first day of Passover and lasted for seven days. It was a feast that remembered and celebrated the day that God led the Israelites out of Egypt. During this time no one was allowed to eat bread with any yeast in it at all, and the house was to be meticulously cleaned to rid it of any trace of yeast.

Yeast is a living organism that is put in the bread to make it rise, which it does by the process of feeding on the bread and then converting (fermentation) its food into carbon dioxide, which thereby "inflated" the dough. Thus Yeast was symbolic of those things that work their ways into our lives and contaminate them—sin. Therefore there was to be absolutely no yeast anywhere, in order to remind and challenge the people of God to remember that he is a pure and holy God and requires them to be pure and holy—without any trace of contamination—as well.

So as the disciples are making the preparations for the Passover meal, this is their backdrop. This is the deep, rich history that they are both a part of and being drawn into. This is their heritage. It is the vivid portrait God had been painting for centuries, in order to show them the full implications of what Jesus, their Passover Lamb, was getting ready to do for them in the days ahead.

Respond:
How do you feel about holidays? How do you celebrate them? What holidays hold significance for you? Why? What do they encourage you to celebrate or remember? What are the days that you celebrate God and what he has done in your life? What will you choose to celebrate and remember about God today?

Rest:
Enjoy this day as a holiday for your soul, in which you rest in that which you celebrate about God today.

Sixty-Seven

Read:

When evening came, Jesus arrived with the Twelve. While they were reclining at the table eating, he said, "Truly I tell you, one of you will betray me—one who is eating with me."

They were saddened, and one by one they said to him, "Surely you don't mean me?"

"It is one of the Twelve," he replied, "one who dips bread into the bowl with me. The Son of Man will go just as it is written about him. But woe to that man who betrays the Son of Man! It would be better for him if he had not been born." (Mark 14:17-21)

Reflect:

Betray [bih-*trey*] – **verb**
1. to deliver or expose to an enemy by treachery or disloyalty.
2. to be unfaithful in guarding, maintaining, or fulfilling.
3. to disappoint the hopes or expectations of; be disloyal to.
4. to reveal or disclose in violation of confidence.
5. to seduce and desert.

Respond:

What does the word *betray* do within you? What does it make you think? How does it make you feel? How would you have taken these words if you had been in the room with Jesus and his disciples? What must Jesus' friends have been feeling and thinking?

And what about Jesus? What was in His heart and on His mind? Do any of the above definitions seem appropriate for Judas? Do any seem appropriate for you?

Rest:

Rest in the love of Jesus that is bigger than all of our mistakes and betrayals.

Sixty-Eight

Read:

While they were eating, Jesus took bread, and when he had given thanks, he broke it and gave it to his disciples, saying, "Take it; this is my body."

Then he took a cup, and when he had given thanks, he gave it to them, and they all drank from it.

"This is my blood of the covenant, which is poured out for many," he said to them. "Truly I tell you, I will not drink again from the fruit of the vine until that day when I drink it new in the kingdom of God."
When they had sung a hymn, they went out to the Mount of Olives. (Mark 14:22-26)

Reflect:

my body
broken
for you

my blood
poured out
for you

do this
and remember
taste deeply
my great affection
for you

eat and drink
feed on me
and be filled
be washed in my blood
and be cleansed
remember my passion
and be convinced
once again
of my great love
for you

Respond:
Spend some time in prayer reflecting on the beauty and the mystery of Jesus' passion as it is revealed in the bread and the wine. What is going on in you? Write it down. And next time you eat the bread and drink the wine…remember.

Rest:
Spend a few minutes resting in His amazing love.

Sixty-Nine

Read:
"You will all fall away," Jesus told them, "for it is written:

> *"'I will strike the shepherd, and the sheep will be scattered.'*

But after I have risen, I will go ahead of you into Galilee."
Peter declared, "Even if all fall away, I will not."
"Truly I tell you," Jesus answered, "today—yes, tonight—before the rooster crows twice you yourself will disown me three times."
But Peter insisted emphatically, "Even if I have to die with you, I will never disown you." And all the others said the same. (Mark 14:27-31)

Reflect:
Did you see *it*? Obviously, neither did the disciples. They were so consumed and preoccupied with their own circumstances and agendas that they never heard *it*. Jesus' first comments about everyone *falling away* had stopped them in their tracks, so much so that they never heard *it*.

That's often the way it is in life. If you aren't really paying careful attention, it is so easy to *miss it*—to miss what God is really saying, to miss what He is really up to. We miss His bigger picture because we are focused in so narrowly on our own smaller picture.

But after I have risen, I will go ahead of you into Galilee. There *it* is. And they never even heard *it*. Jesus was clearly telling them some earth-shattering, life-altering news and they just missed it. It is almost as if Jesus was trying to say, "I'm up to something so much bigger than any of you, if only you will pay attention and not be so consumed with all your own stuff."

I know that in my life oftentimes it is so easy to get consumed with my own agendas, fears, and insecurities that I just lose perspective and miss *it*. I miss what God is trying to do. And I miss what God is trying to say. And I miss where God is trying to lead. What about you?

Respond:
What is the biggest obstacle to you being able to really pay attention to God? How might you combat or overcome that particular obstacle?

Rest:
Just be still and quiet before the Lord for 5 minutes, trying to pay attention to anything He might have to say to you.

Seventy

Read:

They went to a place called Gethsemane, and Jesus said to his disciples, "Sit here while I pray." (Mark 14:32)

Reflect:

Place is so important in the spiritual life. Especially in terms of having a place that is specifically set aside for prayer and silence. Everyone desperately needs just such a place; and Gethsemane was that place for Jesus and his disciples. It was a beautiful and peaceful garden where they retreated often to both rest and pray.

And in his final hours, it is the one place that Jesus runs to. It is the one place where he most longs to be. It is his special place, the place where he and his Father have spent countless hours together. It is a place of comfort and of peace. So here, when Jesus is in his time of deepest need and greatest distress, he goes, with a few of his dearest friends, to this place...to simply be with his Father.

Respond:

Do you have a place? A place set aside for you and God alone? A place you can run to in joy and in sorrow? A place where you go when you are in need of rest and prayer and peace? If not, spend some time this week trying to find that place. And when you find it, go and be with Jesus. Just sit and be with him.

Rest:

Spend the next ten minutes practicing the art of sitting with Jesus.

Seventy-One

Read:

He took Peter, James and John along with him, and he began to be deeply distressed and troubled. "My soul is overwhelmed with sorrow to the point of death," he said to them. "Stay here and keep watch." (Mark 14:33-34)

Reflect:

Are you ever tempted to think that God can't possibly understand the pain and brokenness you've gone through in your life? Are you ever tempted to believe that he can't possibly know what it feels like to be abandoned, or abused, or alone?

Then look no further than this passage. Take a good, long look at the depth of his struggle. Take time to really consider the fragile state of his heart and soul. Behold the sorrow and despair. The road ahead of him is a foreboding one to say the least. He faces pain and struggle, torture and abuse, darkness and despair, abandonment and loneliness that even the most broken among us can hardly imagine.

This is the mystery of the incarnation; that for some unfathomable reason God chooses to enter in to our pain. He himself steps down out of the throne room of heaven and enters our broken and hurting world—drinking deeply of all of its sorrow and sadness and suffering. Why in the world would God choose to do this? It could only be because of his great love for us.

Therefore, it is actually in the times when we are most apt to ask the hard questions, when God's presence has the potential to be the most real and the most tangible. Questions like: "Where is God in the midst of a world that is incredibly broken and pain-filled? Does He even care? Can he really understand the depth of my loneliness, brokenness, and despair?" How is it that God can be the most real and tangible in the midst of these desperate times?

It is only because he has been there. He understands. He has been to the bottom of the pit of darkness and despair. And the whole reason he has gone there is for us. So that he might be able, like no other, to stand with us in the midst of it all and offer us the possibility of hope, healing, and wholeness.

He knows the depths of our pain, so he knows how best to be with us in the midst of it. He knows the depths of our darkness. Therefore, He can redeem it and make it into something that is able to turn us into the people he dreamt for us to be.

Respond:
What do you do with your suffering, sorrow, and pain? Does it make you wonder? Does it cause you to question? Does it drive you toward God or make you want to run away? Why? What does it do within you to know that God entered into suffering and pain for you? What is your response to that?

Rest:
Does he care? The answer is a resounding, "Yes!" He does care. And He intimately understands. If you are looking for Him in brokenness and pain, know that the place that He can always be found is right in the middle of it. Simply be with Jesus in the midst of your pain, whatever it may be. Know that sickness and death and suffering and sorrow do not have the last word—Life does!

Seventy-Two

Read:

Going a little farther, he fell to the ground and prayed that if possible the hour might pass from him. "Abba, Father," he said, "everything is possible for you. Take this cup from me. Yet not what I will, but what you will." (Mark 14:35-36)

Reflect:

If we are completely honest, we all have to admit that we have more questions and uncertainties than we have answers; especially when it comes to the subject of prayer. We realize that prayer is of utmost importance in the spiritual life, and that it is our main avenue for intimate union with our God and Father. But while we realize these truths, we are at a bit of a loss to know exactly how to pray. How are we to go about it? How are we to grow in the art of prayer; and make prayer a vibrant reality and vital part of our relationship with God? That, as usual, is where Jesus comes in. Thankfully he gives us both his life and his Word as faithful guides in this all-important area.

The first thing we notice, as we look to Jesus as our guide for prayer, is that he always turned toward God in every circumstance; not only in his joy, but now also in his deep sorrow, sadness, and despair. In his hour of deepest need, He turns to his Father; he simply runs to God. He desires to be with his Father more than he desires anything else.

In fact, Jesus called God his *Abba*—daddy. It is a term that shows the level of comfort and safety and trust and intimacy that Jesus had with God. God was more than just a distant and powerful figure, God was his papa. It is a term of great tenderness and affection; a term that expresses a deep understanding of what it means to be The Beloved.

Prayer, at its essence, is a place of intimacy where we are fully known and fully loved. It is a place where we become convinced of God's heart for us and of our identity before (and within) him. And once we understand both who God is and who we are, we are able to, as Jesus did, completely trust him with all of our hearts and with all of our lives and with all of our circumstances.

It is because Jesus knew the depths of God's heart that he was able to pray the prayer that follows, *"Take this cup from me. Yet not what I will, but what you will."* Only one who is *convinced* of God's goodness and love and power is able to pray in that way—to pray for His will, rather than our own, to be done.

Respond:

What has your experience of prayer? Is it something you enjoy or struggle with? Why? How would you define prayer? In what ways would changing your view of what prayer really is change your desire or ability to pray? Spend the next 30 minutes in prayer. For the first 10 minutes pour out the depths of your heart to God—let it all out. Then for the next 10 minutes sit and listen to God as he pours out the depths of his heart to you.

Rest:
Now spend your last 10 minutes just being with God—no words at all. Do you realize that each of these 10 minute segments has been prayer?

Seventy-Three

Read:
Then he returned to his disciples and found them sleeping. "Simon," he said to Peter, "are you asleep? Couldn't you keep watch for one hour? Watch and pray so that you will not fall into temptation. The spirit is willing, but the flesh is weak."
Once more he went away and prayed the same thing. When he came back, he again found them sleeping, because their eyes were heavy. They did not know what to say to him.
Returning the third time, he said to them, "Are you still sleeping and resting? Enough! The hour has come. Look, the Son of Man is delivered into the hands of sinners. Rise! Let us go! Here comes my betrayer!"
(Mark 14:37-42)

Reflect:
Are you asleep? Couldn't you keep watch for one hour?
One of the biggest enemies of our spiritual lives is slumber. It was true for the first disciples and it is true for us as well. There are so many times and places and ways that Jesus longs for us to be with him in a way that forms and molds and teaches us, but we are simply not paying attention. We're too busy or too tired or too consumed with other things—too occupied or preoccupied. We are simply asleep.
It may not feel like sleep, or slumber, because it's a life that is so very full of stuff, so active, so scheduled, so very different from our idea of slumber—or of what the disciples appear to be experiencing at this moment. But it is, indeed, the same. It is a spiritual state of being, in which we are completely inattentive and unresponsive. It is slumber. We have been lulled into a spiritual sleep by the noise, and the chaos, and the busyness, and the pace of our own lives. We have missed the *one thing* in pursuit of the *many things* (Luke 10:41-42).
Jesus is not really asking for a lot here. All he is asking of us is to *keep watch*; to *stay awake*, to be *with him*. He just wants us to live in a constant awareness of his presence both within us and around us. He has so much he wants to show us, so much he wants us to know of his love and his heart…if we will just *keep watch*.

Respond:
Before you go to bed tonight take 15 minutes and take a walk with Jesus back through your day. What all happened? What made you smile? What made you laugh? What made you frustrated? What made you sad? What was God up to? Where was God at work that you might have missed at the moment? This is an ancient practice called the Prayer of Examen. Practice it often. It is a helpful way of becoming more awake—aware and attentive to the movement of God in your life.

Rest:
Spend a few minutes resting in the God who is at work at all times, even when we are asleep.

Seventy-Four

Read:
Just as he was speaking, Judas, one of the Twelve, appeared. With him was a crowd armed with swords and clubs, sent from the chief priests, the teachers of the law, and the elders.

Now the betrayer had arranged a signal with them: "The one I kiss is the man; arrest him and lead him away under guard." Going at once to Jesus, Judas said, "Rabbi!" and kissed him. The men seized Jesus and arrested him. Then one of those standing near drew his sword and struck the servant of the high priest, cutting off his ear.

"Am I leading a rebellion," said Jesus, "that you have come out with swords and clubs to capture me? Every day I was with you, teaching in the temple courts, and you did not arrest me. But the Scriptures must be fulfilled." Then everyone deserted him and fled.

A young man, wearing nothing but a linen garment, was following Jesus. When they seized him, he fled naked, leaving his garment behind. (Mark 14:43-52)

Reflect:
There was once a young couple who was deeply in love and had decided to marry. A few weeks after a beautiful wedding and an incredible honeymoon, they had settled in and begun the process of crafting their new life together. It was everything they'd ever dreamed. But before too long the new, young wife began experiencing a strange dizziness and a slurring of her speech. It was soon discovered that she had a tumor in her brain that was growing daily and had to be removed.

The surgeon met often with the young couple before the surgery, explaining in detail all that the surgery would involve, and telling them of both his highest hopes and the greatest risks of such a procedure; one of which could be partial paralysis of one side of her face due to the tumor's proximity to a nerve that controlled many of her facial movements. So in hopes of extending their days on earth together as long as possible, they decided to go through with it.

The day of the surgery came, and the procedure was completed. The young couple sat together in the recovery room anxiously awaiting word from the doctor as to the success of the operation. The good news was that the tumor was removed and the prognosis for the future was very good. The bad news was that, indeed, during the procedure—in order to get the entire tumor—a nerve was damaged that would forever alter the smile of this beautiful young woman.

The young wife was torn: so thankful for the success of the surgery, yet inwardly devastated to learn that her face, from this day forward, would always be contorted; and that her beautiful smile would be permanently disfigured as a result of the operation.

The young husband was simply wonderful in his love for and affirmation of his new bride's beauty as she dealt with the hard news. "I think it looks cute," he said, "I wouldn't change a thing." And as tears streamed down both of their faces he leaned over to kiss his bride gently on her newly disfigured lips. And as he did he twisted his own mouth to fit hers in order to show her that *their kiss still worked*.

It is hard to imagine a better description than that could be given of what God truly did for us in Christ Jesus. Jesus takes on our own deformity. God twists his own mouth to match ours in order to show us that, no matter how distorted and disfigured we have become because of sin, through Him—through the cross—our kiss still works. The cross of Christ is God's kiss.

And is it not incredibly ironic that Judas, the betrayer, would greet this same Jesus in the garden…with a kiss? How amazing, that although he is betrayed, arrested, and soon to be deserted, Jesus still receives this twisted kiss from his "friend" in order to make a way for us all to receive the ultimate kiss of the Father.

Respond:
In what ways is your life twisted, or distorted, or disfigured right now? What would it look like for you to receive the kiss from God's twisted mouth this day; a kiss that shows you his great love and forgiveness, a kiss that brings the dead to life and makes the broken whole once again? Will you receive it? Will you kiss the Son in love and gratitude? Or would you kiss him in betrayal?

Rest:
Receive God's kiss upon your twisted lips today. Rest in his great love and forgiveness.

Seventy-Five

Read:

They took Jesus to the high priest, and all the chief priests, the elders and the teachers of the law came together. Peter followed him at a distance, right into the courtyard of the high priest. There he sat with the guards and warmed himself at the fire. (Mark 14:53-54)

Reflect:

Peter followed him at a distance...

Is it really possible to truly follow Jesus and *follow him at a distance*? I mean really? I know we'd all like to believe it is. For the most part many of us want to be close enough to get the benefits of the life Jesus offers without having to pay the high cost involved in truly following him. In the words of a writer from long ago, "It is as if we want to get close enough to warm our hands by the fire of his love, but not close enough to be totally consumed [and transformed] by the flames of His holiness."

Peter's reason for following at a distance was simple—fear. It is the same fear which would later cause him to deny that he even knew Jesus at all. What was it that he was most afraid of? Was it fear for his own safety? Or did it have to do more with his reputation? Was the issue acceptance? Or could it have been popularity? If you were in his shoes what would you have been most afraid of? How does fear make you distance yourself from Jesus?

Respond:

In what ways are you following Jesus at a distance? How? Why? Draw a picture of your relationship with Jesus right now. As you look at the picture, what do you notice? Now draw a picture of what you wish your relationship with Jesus looked like. Hold these pictures before God in prayer and ask him for the courage to truly follow Jesus.

Rest:

Run to the strong tower of Jesus (Proverbs 18:10) and be safe from all of your fears. Spend a few minutes resting in him.

Seventy-Six

Read:

The chief priests and the whole Sanhedrin were looking for evidence against Jesus so that they could put him to death, but they did not find any. Many testified falsely against him, but their statements did not agree.

Then some stood up and gave this false testimony against him: "We heard him say, 'I will destroy this temple made with human hands and in three days will build another, not made with hands.'" Yet even then their testimony did not agree.

Then the high priest stood up before them and asked Jesus, "Are you not going to answer? What is this testimony that these men are bringing against you?" But Jesus remained silent and gave no answer.

Again the high priest asked him, "Are you the Messiah, the Son of the Blessed One?"

"I am," said Jesus. "And you will see the Son of Man sitting at the right hand of the Mighty One and coming on the clouds of heaven."

The high priest tore his clothes. "Why do we need any more witnesses?" he asked. "You have heard the blasphemy. What do you think?"

They all condemned him as worthy of death. Then some began to spit at him; they blindfolded him, struck him with their fists, and said, "Prophesy!" And the guards took him and beat him. (Mark 14:55-65)

Reflect:
Are you the Messiah, the Son of the Blessed One?

Wouldn't you think that the person asking this question would be doing so out of a hopeful, curious, sense of excitement and anticipation? I mean look at the question. It asks if Jesus is THE ONE. Are you the One we have been waiting on for hundreds of years? Are you the One who will come to save us, redeem us, and set us free? Are you the Messiah—the promised and expected deliverer? Are you the Son of the Blessed One— the Son of God Most High? Wouldn't you think they would be desperately hoping the answer would be yes, if they were truly looking for, and longing for, God to finally show up?

But their reaction shows that his answer wasn't really the answer they were looking for. They were not really hoping for Almighty God to come and live among his people at all. They were just worried about their own interests; and defending their own territory. They didn't really want Almighty God, they just wanted a puppet that they could control. They were only interested in a god that would keep them in power and not alter the way of life they had become so used to and comfortable with. They loved their power, their comfort, and their control. They loved their own agenda much more than they ever loved God. They were okay with God showing up as long as he didn't "upset their apple cart."

But that's exactly what Jesus did. He wasn't what they were looking for at all. Instead of being compliant, he was radical. Instead of be controlled, he was turning things upside down. Instead of going along with their agenda, he was upsetting the status quo; and something had to be done about it.

So they sprang into action. They arrested the Holy One of God and put him on trial. They bound the hands of the Prince of Peace. They spit in the face of the King of Kings. And they blindfolded, mocked, struck, and beat the Son of the Blessed One. And Jesus, God's Beloved Son, took it all...for you and me.

Respond:
Stand in the crowd and watch the proceedings. Listen to the voices. Watch the actions. Why the anger? Why do you think they feel so threatened? What are they so afraid of? Where are you in this scene? What is going on in your heart as you see all of this being done? What do you want to do? What do you want to say to Him? Write about it in your journal.

Rest:
Rest in the presence of Jesus; who loves you enough to endure all of this abuse for you.

Seventy-Seven

Read:
While Peter was below in the courtyard, one of the servant girls of the high priest came by. When she saw Peter warming himself, she looked closely at him.

"You also were with that Nazarene, Jesus," she said.

But he denied it. "I don't know or understand what you're talking about," he said, and went out into the entryway.

When the servant girl saw him there, she said again to those standing around, "This fellow is one of them." Again he denied it.

After a little while, those standing near said to Peter, "Surely you are one of them, for you are a Galilean."

He began to call down curses, and he swore to them, "I don't know this man you're talking about."

Immediately the rooster crowed the second time. Then Peter remembered the word Jesus had spoken to him: "Before the rooster crows twice you will disown me three times." And he broke down and wept. (Mark 14:66-72)

Reflect:
Have you ever completely blown it? Have you ever been in a situation where you disappointed or hurt someone so deeply that you doubted if your relationship could ever be the same again? After all, you had done something so horrible and/or so hurtful that you couldn't (and wouldn't) blame them (those you'd hurt) if they never spoke to you again, much less ever forgave you.

Can you remember the guilt and the shame? Can you remember the tears? They were tears that poured down your face, but felt as though they were pouring right out of the depths of your broken heart. These were the kind of tears that Peter shed on this particular night. They were tears of regret and remorse, tears of disgrace and humiliation, tears of indescribable pain and self-contempt—total and complete brokenness. I'm sure he was tempted to believe that it was all over, that there was no hope, no way back. He had made a complete mess out of everything.

If you have ever been in this terrible place, fear not. Do not despair. There is hope. There is amazing news just ahead. The news is that Jesus does some of his best work in the midst of the mess. In fact, Jesus specializes in folks just like me and you.

Rest:

Rest in the fact that Jesus accepts you, mess and all, right where you are. And he longs to wrap his arms of love around you, cleanse your heart, and give you hope.

Seventy-Eight

Read:

Very early in the morning, the chief priests, with the elders, the teachers of the law and the whole Sanhedrin, made their plans. So they bound Jesus, led him away and handed him over to Pilate.

"Are you the king of the Jews?" asked Pilate.

"You have said so," Jesus replied.

The chief priests accused him of many things. So again Pilate asked him, "Aren't you going to answer? See how many things they are accusing you of."

But Jesus still made no reply, and Pilate was amazed. (Mark 15:1-5)

Reflect:

Pilate had been around the block a time or two. He had seen a lot of things in his time ruling over Jerusalem. But Pilate had never seen anything quite like this. Many had been brought before him through the years, yet none of them was like this man. None of them had had the impact on peoples lives that this man seemed to have. None had aroused the kind of passion he seemed to arouse or caused the commotion he seemed to cause. None had been so harshly accused by the religious experts. And none had remained silent in the face of those accusations.

In fact, as Jesus stood before Pilate, it was almost as if he had no need to say a single word. He was totally at peace. And even as the religious leaders attacked and attacked, what did Jesus do in return? Did he resist? Did he defend? Did he explain? Did he retaliate? No, he did none of the above. He simply remained silent. He didn't say a word. He *made no reply...and Pilate was amazed.*

What do you think it was that amazed him so? If you were Pilate, what would have amazed you the most?

Respond:
What amazes you most about Jesus? What would you have done as you stood before Pilate? How is his reaction a model for you? Is there a place in your life where you are you tempted to resist, or defend, or explain, or retaliate? What would it look like to follow Jesus' example instead?

Rest:
Spend a few minutes resting in God's amazing presence.

Seventy-Nine

Read:
Now it was the custom at the festival to release a prisoner whom the people requested. A man called Barabbas was in prison with the insurrectionists who had committed murder in the uprising. The crowd came up and asked Pilate to do for them what he usually did.

"Do you want me to release to you the king of the Jews?" asked Pilate, knowing it was out of self-interest that the chief priests had handed Jesus over to him. But the chief priests stirred up the crowd to have Pilate release Barabbas instead.

"What shall I do, then, with the one you call the king of the Jews?" Pilate asked them.

"Crucify him!" they shouted.

"Why? What crime has he committed?" asked Pilate.

But they shouted all the louder, "Crucify him!"

Wanting to satisfy the crowd, Pilate released Barabbas to them. He had Jesus flogged, and handed him over to be crucified. (Mark 15:6-15)

Reflect:
He took my place. That is the thought that fills my heart and my mind both day and night. I just can't stop thinking about it. I just can't stop thinking about *him.* I was the one that deserved to die. I was the one who was guilty. I was the murderer.

Yet *he took my place.* He did absolutely nothing wrong; nothing worthy of death. He was totally innocent. Yet he took the punishment that was rightly mine. I am the one who should be nailed to that cross. I am the one that should be hanging on that tree—not him. Yet there he is, dying a criminal's death, in my place.

They say his name is Jesus—*Yeshua*—which means to deliver, to save, or to rescue. That name could not be more fitting, for that is exactly what he has done for *me*. And my name is Barabbas: *bar* meaning son of and *abba* meaning daddy, or papa. Jesus (*Yeshua*) rescued me, so that I (*Barabbas*) could become a son of the Father. *He took my place.* so that I could come home; home to my Father—the One who made me and the One who loves me dearly...and because of that, my life will never be the same.

Respond:
Read the story of the cross (Mark 15) once again, with the realization that *that should be me*. Then write a letter to Jesus thanking him for *taking your place*.

Rest:
Just spend some time being with Jesus, in gratitude for what he has done for you.

Eighty

Read:
The soldiers led Jesus away into the palace (that is, the Praetorium) and called together the whole company of soldiers. They put a purple robe on him, then twisted together a crown of thorns and set it on him. And they began to call out to him, "Hail, king of the Jews!" Again and again they struck him on the head with a staff and spit on him. Falling on their knees, they paid homage to him. And when they had mocked him, they took off the purple robe and put his own clothes on him. Then they led him out to crucify him. (Mark 15:16-20)

Reflect:
For most of last three years of Jesus' life on earth he spent his days doing things for (or "unto") other people—in the very best sense of the word. And now, during his final hours, the focus shifts from doing things for others to having things done to (or "unto") him. He goes from loving the lost, and healing the broken, and raising the dead to being mocked, and beaten, and eventually crucified.

Can you imagine—if you were Jesus—allowing those, whom you had lovingly created, to do such horrible things "unto" you? Look at the scene above and imagine that you were Jesus—God in the flesh. What would you do? Would you be able to allow these things to be "done unto" you? Or would you give these people the full measure of what they really deserve?

And as we look at this scene, we must realize that it is not just this random group of people doing things "unto" Jesus…it is us. It is our sin that makes it all necessary. It is our rebellion that is the whole reason for it all. Each time we turn away from the Living God and go our own way, we are the ones that reject and ridicule Jesus. We are the ones that drive the thorns into his brow. We are the ones pounding the nails into his hands and feet. We are the ones putting him on the cross to die the death of a common criminal.

Respond:
Put yourself in the scene above. Where are you? What do you see? How does it make you feel? What do you want to say to Jesus right now?

Rest:
Rest in the loving arms of the God who is willing to be "done unto" because of his great love for you.

Eighty-One

Read:
A certain man from Cyrene, Simon, the father of Alexander and Rufus, was passing by on his way in from the country, and they forced him to carry the cross. They brought Jesus to the place called Golgotha (which means "the place of the skull"). Then they offered him wine mixed with myrrh, but he did not take it. And they crucified him. Dividing up his clothes, they cast lots to see what each would get.

It was nine in the morning when they crucified him. The written notice of the charge against him read: THE KING OF THE JEWS.

They crucified two rebels with him, one on his right and one on his left. Those who passed by hurled insults at him, shaking their heads and saying, "So! You who are going to destroy the temple and build it in three days, come down from the cross and save yourself!" In the same way the chief priests and the teachers of the law mocked him among themselves. "He saved others," they said, "but he can't save himself! Let this Messiah, this king of Israel, come down now from the cross, that we may see and believe." Those crucified with him also heaped insults on him. (Mark 15:21-32)

Reflect:
What an agonizing scene. The Son of the Most High God nailed to a cross—stripped, mocked, and insulted. The King of Kings becoming the object of jeers and abuse; struggling for each breath, in excruciating pain. It is just so hard to watch.

And harder, I am sure, to endure. Just imagine having the power to do exactly what the taunts aimed at you were calling for—to *save yourself* and to *come down from the cross*—and not doing it. Imagine the restraint. Imagine the patience. Imagine the self-control. Imagine the love; love so great that you are able to not lash out at those inflicting all of this damage upon you, but actually offer them salvation.

Respond:
Spend a few minutes standing at the foot of the cross again…watching. What do you see? Look at the face of Jesus. What is in his eyes? Imagine what is in his heart? Draw a picture of what you see.

Rest:
Spend a few minutes just being with Jesus, receiving the love he is showering upon you. Allow his blood to wash you clean.

Eighty-Two

Read:
At noon, darkness came over the whole land until three in the afternoon. (Mark 15:33)

Reflect:
It is humanity's darkest hour. So dark, in fact, that the sun hid its face in shame for all that had just taken place. For three solid hours it just couldn't bring itself to shine. All of creation stood in stunned silence. God had just been brutally executed by the very people he created to love. And darkness prevailed…or so it seemed.

What in the world was going on? Had all hope been lost? Had darkness been victorious—forever? Or was there something bigger at work here? Or someone? Someone bigger than all of the deepest darkness?

What an incredible mystery: that even when things are their darkest and most desperate, God is still at work. God is always up to something— whether we can see it or not, whether we can sense it or not, whether we can understand it or not. God is mysteriously present. And in spite of the way it might appear at the moment, he can be fully trusted.

After all, what could possibly be darker and more desperate than this? And yet, even here, God is at work—redeeming a lost and broken world.

Respond:
Think back on your life thus far. Was there a time where all seemed dark? In the midst of that dark time, was there any sense that God was up to something that you could neither see nor understand at the moment?

What did God do in you, through you, or for you during that time? How does that help you to trust him more with whatever may come?

Rest:
Rest in our God who brings life and hope, even out of the deepest darkness.

Eighty-Three

Read:
And at three in the afternoon Jesus cried out in a loud voice, "Eloi, Eloi, lema sabachthani?" (which means "My God, my God, why have you forsaken me?").

When some of those standing near heard this, they said, "Listen, he's calling Elijah."

Someone ran, filled a sponge with wine vinegar, put it on a staff, and offered it to Jesus to drink. "Now leave him alone. Let's see if Elijah comes to take him down," he said. (Mark 15:34-36)

Reflect:
My God, my God, why have you forsaken me?

What a question! It is as raw and as real as it gets; but it is also straight from the Scriptures—Psalm 22:1. Was Jesus relying on the Word in his moment of greatest need? Or was God showing us his amazing power and intentionality by recording the very thoughts and feelings of Jesus on the cross hundreds of years before it happens? Wouldn't it be just like God to do that?

In either case, it is a desperate cry—one filled with pain, abandonment, and loneliness. It is, in fact, the only place in the New Testament where Jesus does not refer to God as his Father...but as *My God, My God!* What is the significance of this cry? How are we to understand it? What is really going on here? Obviously those standing nearby had absolutely no idea: just look at their reaction.

The significance of it all has to do with the idea of *separation*. Jesus is separated from God. For the very first time, in eternity past, the Son is mysteriously cut off from the Father he has always been in intimate union with. He is estranged, apart, alone. And the sole reason for this separation is sin—our sin. Jesus takes upon himself our sin, and our rebellion, and our lawlessness, as well as our separation from God.

"My God, my God, why have you forsaken me?" This is the resulting cry, which comes up from the depths of his heart and soul. Jesus chooses to become forsaken by his Father so that we might have relationship with God once again. God the Father turns away from his beloved Son

because he was covered with the repulsive filth of our sin; sin that he, in his holiness, could not tolerate the presence of.

Response:
Reflect on the words *"My God, my God, why have you forsaken me?"* Repeat them to yourself over and over again. Stand at the foot of the cross and listen to them come from the lips of our Savior. What is his tone? What is the expression on his face? Imagine what is in his heart. What does hearing these words coming from his lips do within you? What do you want to say to Jesus in response? Write it all in your journal.

Rest:
Rest in the love and presence of the Father from which (through Jesus) nothing can ever separate you.

Eighty-Four

Read:
> With a loud cry, Jesus breathed his last. (Mark 15:37)

Reflect:
Finishing. It's arguably the most important part of just about anything—be it race, game, or journey. Sure it's vital to get off to a good start in whatever you may be undertaking; and just as vital to plug away diligently in the middle of "it"—whatever "it" may be. But how you finish is the most significant part; because how you finish has to do with arriving at your chosen destination. The way you finish is what's remembered most; what determines your result or successfulness.

We are a culture of such poor finishers. Our lives are filled with blown diets, abandoned exercise programs, unfinished home improvement projects, half-read books, etc. We have trouble setting our resolve, keeping our motivation, sustaining our direction, and staying the course. As a result, when circumstances get hard, or the going gets tough, or things don't exactly go our way…we quit. We simply give up, fizzle out, or stop trying.

It is finished! These are the very last words uttered by Jesus from the cross (John 19:30). They are words filled with meaning and significance. They are words of victory rather than defeat—of a mission that has been accomplished, or a job that has been completed, or a debt that has been covered. In fact, they are the very words that were stamped on a *certificate of debt* once it had been paid in full.

Jesus had finished, and finished well…Thanks be to God! Maybe it was not the finish most of his disciples had imagined, or even hoped for, but it was exactly the way that the Father had it all planned. Jesus had done it, he had completed his mission, he had fulfilled his purpose. It was finished; in spite of all the obstacles and all the suffering and all the pain. It was finished; in spite of the extreme nature of his Divine mission. It was finished. And aren't you so grateful? Grateful that Jesus is a much better finisher than we are.

Respond:
How do you feel when you have finished something? When you have completed a difficult, yet rewarding task? Are you relieved? Satisfied? Joyful? At peace? Is there a sense of accomplishment, or celebration? Where have you finished well?

Now consider the places in your life where haven't finished well. What is God saying to you about these? Does seeing Jesus finish well give you the power and the motivation to finish well yourself?

Rest:
Rest in what Jesus has finished for you. There is not a thing you can—or have to—do to add to what he has finished. It is done.

Eighty-Five

Read:
The curtain of the temple was torn in two from top to bottom. (Mark 15:38)

Reflect:
The curtain was such a significant part of the Temple structure. It was what separated the place where the priests performed their duties, from the Holy of Holies; where only the High Priest could go, and that only once a year on the Day of Atonement. The Holy of Holies represented the very presence of God; it was THE place where God dwelt. Thus, the curtain was what separated the Holy God from sinful man.

And now, as Jesus dies upon the cross, that separation is removed. The curtain of the Temple is torn into; not in some haphazard way, but from top to bottom—from heaven to earth. It is as if God's own hands reached down out of heaven and did for man what he could not possibly do for himself—open up the way back to God. And so, through the cross, now the way to God is wide open—because of Jesus.

Respond:
What curtains are there in your life? How do they separate you from God? On a sheet of paper, write down all of the things in your heart and life that give you a sense of separation from God. Take your time and make sure you write down everything that comes to mind. When you have completed

the list, in very large letters write the words "It is finished" over it all. Now take the piece of paper and tear it in to, from top to bottom. This is what Jesus has done for you—you are no longer separated from the Father. Give thanks to Jesus for his work on the cross.

Rest:
Spend a few minutes resting in your forgiveness, in the fact that there is now no more separation, and you can come into the very presence of God.

Eighty-Six

Read:
And when the centurion, who stood there in front of Jesus, saw how he died, he said, "Surely this man was the Son of God!" (Mark 15:39)

Reflect:
A centurion was a Roman soldier, of equivalent rank to a regimental sergeant major. He was in charge of 100 men. To have risen to this rank he was most assuredly a man of experience, a true veteran of war; which means he would've been a hardened soldier who had fought in battles more numerous than he could count, and had seen more men die than he could possibly remember.

And yet what he was witnessing at this very moment was something he could never forget. Most likely he had seen hundreds of men die, but he had never seen anyone die quite like this. Never had he seen a man willingly lay down his arms to the driving of the nails. Never had he seen a man praying for the forgiveness of those who were putting him to death. Never had he seen the sky grow as dark as night in the middle of the day. Never had he seen a man so full of grace and mercy and love, in the face of such abuse and torture and ridicule.

And as he watched the passion of Jesus unfold, he was swept up in the beauty and the tragedy of it all. In fact, he was profoundly impacted, transformed, changed forever. He had likely watched many crucifixions— seen many men die on a cross—but there was something profoundly different about this one. There was something *more* to this one. There was something *bigger* at work here. What in the world was it? Could it really be that this man was exactly who he said he was? Could he really be the Son of God?

Respond:
Stand at the foot of the cross once again today and witness all that the centurion witnessed. What impacts you the most? What about the cross makes you proclaim, "Surely this man is the Son of God"?

Rest:
Take a few minutes and rest in the work and the beauty of the cross.

Eighty-Seven

Read:
Some women were watching from a distance. Among them were Mary Magdalene, Mary the mother of James the younger and of Joseph, and Salome. In Galilee these women had followed him and cared for his needs. Many other women who had come up with him to Jerusalem were also there. (Mark 15:40-41)

Reflect:

He had taken their hearts captive
they just couldn't leave
love wouldn't allow it
so they stood
and watched from a distance
as their beloved Jesus
breathed his last

There was nowhere else they could be
except as near to him as possible
they had been with him all along
doing whatever they could
meeting whatever needs arose
they would do anything for him
nothing was too small
or too large
for the enormous affection
that dwelt within them

he held their hearts
in his strong and tender hands
now cut deep with wounds
hewn by nails
revealing a love
more pure and true and deep
than any they had ever known
a love beyond limits

This love had captured them
completely
and from now on

all that they had
and all that they were
belonged only to him.

Respond:
How do you express your love and devotion to Jesus? What would you do to show him you love him? Ask Jesus how he desires you to show him your affection. He has called you his Beloved, will you call him yours?

Rest:
Simply spend a few minutes in the presence of your beloved Jesus.

Eighty-Eight

Read:
It was Preparation Day (that is, the day before the Sabbath). So as evening approached, Joseph of Arimathea, a prominent member of the Council, who was himself waiting for the kingdom of God, went boldly to Pilate and asked for Jesus' body. Pilate was surprised to hear that he was already dead. Summoning the centurion, he asked him if Jesus had already died. When he learned from the centurion that it was so, he gave the body to Joseph. So Joseph bought some linen cloth, took down the body, wrapped it in the linen, and placed it in a tomb cut out of rock. Then he rolled a stone against the entrance of the tomb. Mary Magdalene and Mary the mother of Joseph saw where he was laid. (Mark 15:42-47)

Reflect:
Joseph was *a prominent member of the Council*. He had also *become a disciple of Jesus* (Matthew 27:57); but a disciple *secretly because of fear of the Jews* (John 19:38). He was a *good and upright man, who had not consented to their decision and action* concerning Jesus (Luke 23:50). But most of all Joseph of Arimathea *was himself waiting for the kingdom of God.*

What does that statement really mean? What does it mean to wait for the kingdom of God? Does it simply mean that Joseph was waiting and watching, like all of his Jewish colleagues, for the Messiah to appear at some mysterious day and time? Or does it insinuate that Joseph knew, as Jesus had proclaimed, that the kingdom of God was indeed *at hand*?

Did he realize that since the King was in his kingdom, that the kingdom of God had indeed already arrived among them? And what exactly is the difference? How does it change our thinking and our seeing and our living to believe that the kingdom of God is a current reality rather than just a future hope?

For Joseph it meant that he couldn't remain the same any longer, he had to live life differently. Since the kingdom of God was at hand, he must live by kingdom rule rather than by his own plan and agenda. Living by kingdom rule meant that he could not live for his own safety and comfort any longer. He could not remain a secret disciple for one more second. Life with Jesus *had to* become his first priority. Any other version of spiritual life was just an illusion. His life was proof that his heart had been captured by his love for the King. So he had to step forward, out of the shadows, and show what was truly most important in his life and heart.

And it is the same for each of us. The spiritual life is, first of all, a life. It is not a one-time decision, or the walking of an aisle, or the raising of a hand, or even the saying of a prayer. It is a life. It is a life lived for the King—in the kingdom of God. It is a life where our love for and our allegiance to Jesus defines us, and determines everything about us.

Respond:
What does the kingdom of God mean to you? Is it something you are waiting for or living in the midst of? Is it only a future hope? Or is it a present reality? This very day how would your life be different if you lived every second of it as if the kingdom of God was at hand? As if the King was present in the kingdom?

Rest:
Simply rest for a few minutes in the presence of your King.

Eighty-Nine

Read:
When the Sabbath was over, Mary Magdalene, Mary the mother of James, and Salome bought spices so that they might go to anoint Jesus' body. Very early on the first day of the week, just after sunrise, they were on their way to the tomb and they asked each other, "Who will roll the stone away from the entrance of the tomb?"

But when they looked up, they saw that the stone, which was very large, had been rolled away. As they entered the tomb, they saw a young man dressed in a white robe sitting on the right side, and they were alarmed.

"Don't be alarmed," he said. "You are looking for Jesus the Nazarene, who was crucified. He has risen! He is not here. See the place where they laid him. (Mark 16:1-6)

Reflection:

> the stone lies
> on its side
> rolled away
> easter has
> uttered an

invitation *Rise Up! Come out! Enjoy the light of
new life!* but instead we sit befriending the dark
tomb content with despairing—inertia or gravity

> has taken
> hold so we
> sit and mope
> in the dark
> even though
> the stone lies
> on its side
> rolled away
> (by Jim Branch)

He has risen! He is alive!! And because of that, so are we!!!

Respond:

Find a stone and hold it in your hands. What are the qualities of it?
Imagine a stone so heavy that you couldn't move it at all, no matter how
hard you tried. How does that make you feel?

Consider the stones in your life. What stones are rolled in front of the
entrance to your heart that you simply can't move? What things still hold
you captive to the stench of death and decay? Through his death and
resurrection, Jesus has rolled away those stones and called you out into
new life. Will you step out of the tomb? Will you step into freedom? Or
will you stay in the dark grave and continue to be trapped in bondage to
death?

Rest:

Rest for a few minutes in the presence of the risen Jesus; the one who is
able to move the largest of stones.

Ninety

Read:

> But go, tell his disciples and Peter, 'He is going ahead of you into
> Galilee. There you will see him, just as he told you.'" (Mark 16:7)

Reflect:
...and Peter.

Isn't it just like God to put that in there? How incredibly kind of Him to affirm the one that, no doubt, needed affirmation the most. After all, Peter was the one who had denied Jesus and had, most likely, spent the last couple of days in the agony of personal grief, failure, and moral collapse. "Some rock I am," Peter must've been thinking. "I am such a coward, such a screw up, such a pathetic excuse for a human being, much less a disciple"

Jesus knew it all too well. And because of that, he made sure that the angel passed along a very special message. *Tell the disciples and Peter.* It was almost as if he was telling Peter, "You are not a coward. You are not failure. You are not a screw up. You are still my disciple. You are still my rock. You are still my beloved."

Respond:
Write a paragraph or two about a time when you really failed or disappointed someone you loved deeply? What did it feel like? What were the "tapes" that played in your head? What names did you call yourself? What were you tempted to believe was really true about you? What was your reaction? What did you do? How did you handle it?

Now write a paragraph or two about a time when you felt like you really disappointed Jesus. What was that like? Now imagine that it is you that Jesus is sending a message to, after your failure. What does he want to say to you? What are his words? Know that they are words of love and acceptance; forgiveness and restoration.

Rest:
Simply rest in the words of love and affection and forgiveness that Jesus gave you today.

Ninety-One

Read:
Trembling and bewildered, the women went out and fled from the tomb. They said nothing to anyone, because they were afraid. (Mark 16:8)

Reflect:
Trembling and bewildered and afraid.

Not exactly the best words to end on are they? The women left the tomb not really knowing what to think, not really knowing what to say. So they kept quiet until they got back to the upper room where all the others were gathered. Could it really be? Was he really alive? How can we be sure we weren't just seeing things? How do we know it wasn't all just a dream?

Over the next forty days Jesus would meet them again and again in places and in ways that would leave no doubt in their hearts or minds that he had risen—that he was, indeed, alive—and seemingly, in some ways, more alive than he had ever been. But as they left the tomb—at the beginning of this new season, this new adventure—they were frightened and unsure. And there is something deep within me that is actually glad they were; because I feel that way so much of the time in my own journey.

Even in the times when I am relatively sure I have seen him and I have heard from him, there is still a little fear and uncertainty. There are still times when I am *trembling and bewildered and afraid.* Just knowing that the very ones who saw the empty tomb and heard the words from the angel were that way as well gives me hope; hope that in spite of all of the doubt, uncertainty, and insecurity I might experience along the way, I can still live a life of faith and trust. I don't have to have it all figured out in order to follow Jesus with all my heart.

In many ways the end of Mark's gospel is just a new beginning. Over the next days, weeks, months, and years (all through the book of Acts, as well as the rest of the New Testament) we get to see first-hand how *trembling and bewildered and afraid* is transformed by the Spirit of God into bold and courageous and fearless. These ordinary people, with all of their fears, insecurities and weaknesses, had been marked forever by Jesus; and they would never be the same.

Respond:
What are your biggest fears and your wildest dreams for the journey ahead with Jesus? Write yourself a letter, telling yourself what you hope your life with him will be like a year from now. Put the letter in an envelope, seal it, and write the date exactly one year from now on the front. Give the envelope to a friend and ask him/her to give it to you or send it to your on that date.

Rest:
Spend a few minutes resting in the arms of the Father, who is bigger than all of your deepest fears and your wildest dreams.

Well, that's the end of this leg of our journey together. Thanks for being willing to come along. I pray that it has been a rich and fruitful time for you; I know it has been for me. As one last exercise of prayer, look back on these last weeks and months we have spent together and reflect on all that God has said and done. What are the things that remain with you the most from our time together? Try to name them and take hold of them. Write them all down in your journal. How will these things travel with you and within you in the days, weeks, and months ahead? Thank God for his presence, both in your life and in his Word.

Grace and Peace,
JB

27427494R00068

Made in the USA
Lexington, KY
14 November 2013